Observation Drawing with Children
A Framework for Teachers

Observation Drawing with Children
A Framework for Teachers

Nancy R. Smith and the Drawing Study Group

The Drawing Study Group

Laraine Cicchetti
Margaret C. Clark
Carolee Fucigna
Barbara Gordon-O'Connor
Barbara A. Halley
Margaret Kennedy

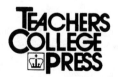

Teachers College, Columbia University
New York and London

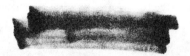

Published by Teachers College Press, 1234 Amsterdam Avenue, New York, N.Y. 10027

Library of Congress Cataloging-in-Publication Data

Smith, Nancy R.
    Observation drawing with children: a framework for teachers/
Nancy R. Smith, and the drawing study group.
        p. cm.
    Includes bibliographical references and index.
    ISBN 0-8077-3692-9 (alk. Paper). — ISBN 0-8077-3691-0
(pbk.: alk. Paper)
    1. Drawing, Psychology of. 2. Learning, Psychology of.   I. Title.
BF723.D7S65 1998
370.15'23—dc21   97-37995

ISBN 0-8077-3691-0 (pbk.)
ISBN 0-8077-3692-9 (cloth)

Printed on acid-free paper

Manufactured in the United States of America

05 04 03 02 01 00 99 98   8 7 6 5 4 3 2 1

We always live at the time we live and not at some other time, and only by extracting at each present time the full meaning of each present experience are we prepared for doing the same thing in the future. This is the only preparation which in the long run amounts to anything. All this means that attentive care must be devoted to the conditions which give each present experience a worthwhile meaning.

—John Dewey, Experience and Education, 1938

Contents

Foreword

DRAWING DEVELOPMENT

Nearly a century ago, Georges-Henri Luquet (1913) made a study of his own daughter's drawings in which he sketched a progression from scribble, to circle, to "tadpole," to human figure. His description has become the almost legendary account of the stages of drawing—it shows up in textbooks on child development, teacher training manuals, and handbooks for new parents. In offering this account, Luquet gave us one of the earliest, most visible, and robust demonstrations of the young child as an active inventor, not just a consumer, of the symbol systems he or she will use throughout the rest of life. But like all other original and powerful descriptions, Luquet's account also locked us into seeing the development of children's drawings in a very particular way. First, Luquet, as well as those that have followed and believed him, left us essentially a romantic portrait of the child as artist. Young children drew what they thought or felt, not what they saw; they portrayed an internal, not an external world. They were too young, or too simple, or too unspoiled to take on the demands of realistic rendition. According to this account, until the age of ten or so, young children could only draw schematically—tadpole figures, stiff-as-cardboard flowers, dogs that look very much like small horses. It is a portrait of the child artist that was nurtured by successive generations of art educators—Cizek, Lowenfeld, and others. In part, this portrait of children as innocent of the world mattered hugely to these teacher–scholars who escaped to the United States and Britain from the prejudice, war, and privation of Central Europe in the turbulent period bounded by World War I and II. The second ingredient in Luquet's view was that drawing development spun out in a series of highly predictable stages through which young children inched closer and closer to realistic rendition: the folds of cloth, the bulges of muscle, the volume of a peach, the handles of a bicycle cocked at an odd angle.

What is both important and exciting about this volume is that it opens our eyes to a view of drawing development as powerful as Luquet's, but radically different. In these pages, 5-, 8-, and 10-year-old children are no longer visual innocents. They draw from observation, setting down the shapes of bicycle wheels and daffodil trumpets, the spines and ribs on cacti, and the sweep and texture of birds' wings. These drawings are anything but the simplified schematizations that the stock-in-trade accounts of drawing development would have told us to expect from young children. In addition, these drawings are outright contradictions to the sequence of stages Luquet and his followers promised us. But, if this is so, how did we fail to notice what acute observers young children could be? Why have we thought that young children, who learn the grammar of native languages by age 5, could never manage to draw the complex visual world of bicycle wheels and bird wings?

The story is an old one. To begin, Luquet's view of drawing development presumes that children's drawings are as partial and schematic as they are because the childlike nature of their minds and hands intervened, preventing them from taking in the world with all its wrinkles, distances, and forms exactly as it is. In addition, Luquet and his colleagues argued that children's drawings evolved towards realism by relying on the basic imagery of human development they inherited from Christian religion and Western literature. That view portrayed all life laid out in one great and ordered chain of being leading assuredly from animal to man, serf to lord to monarch, hell to heaven, primitive to developed cultures, lunatic to rational man, and low to high art. In fact, this image of development as a ladder was so pervasive that competing and more complex images for development, such as Darwin's images of evolutionary change as a branching coral or Freud's view of the mature mind as dreaming *and* thinking, were transformed into the much more rigid language of "lower" and "higher."

The study of children's drawings was no different. In research circles, clinical work, and school entrance testing, the predictable order of the emergence of different forms of human figures from scribble to circle to schematic tadpole figure became law. Three quarters of a century later, even the most active branch of developmental drawing research—studies that argue very young children can use occlusion, foreshortening, and perspective—never questions the fundamental model of a universal, unilinear progression from simple schematic towards realistic drawing (see Freeman & Cox, 1985).

But the most basic assumptions on which Luquet and his colleagues built their original observations have all shifted. First, we no longer think of the eye as a camera, but as an extension of an active mind. Drawing hasn't been "faithful" since Manet's patches of color or Seurat's dots. Recent events in the history of photography and video—once heralded as the most relentlessly neutral and "faithful" of all visual languages—have proven that these media are as highly selective and constructive of reality as Cezanne's drawings or Picasso's paintings ever were. The varying effects of showing videotapes at normal speed and in slow motion, the possibility of inserting fictional characters into historical footage, and the jolt of joining animated figures and live action have yielded a visual culture in which transformation, editing, and merging have replaced recording and reporting as the central acts, even the responsibilities, of graphic representations.

In addition, the bedrock hierarchies that once ordered the arts of different cultures from primitive to developed, that graded art forms from low to high, and that classified heritage and folk arts "beneath" refined portraiture and sculpture have all been questioned, if not toppled. Aboriginal paintings, Mickey Mouse, advertising imagery, and quilts, all once invisible, are very much the stuff of museum exhibitions, auctions, and reviews, independent of any attempt to create a believable illusionary realm within a frame (Danto, 1994; Varnedoe & Gopnik, 1990).

Once we acknowledge a visual world where realism is only one, rather than the single imperial, option, we can at last understand a double message that artists and artist-teachers like those writing in this book have been trying to deliver: We misunderstand drawing profoundly to the extent that we imagine that proficiency at representing volumes and distances is drawing's first and most consuming purpose, or crowning achievement. And to the extent that you believe children draw in order to "re-photograph" the world, you will never understand what compels a young person to look closely, to experiment with marks, or to be pleased or broken-hearted by what takes shape (Clark, 1995; Pariser, 1995; Wilson & Wilson, 1977; Wolf & Perry, 1988).

Second, our views of human development have changed profoundly. The sturdy and purportedly stable architecture of stages (the developmental version of the great chain of being) has been challenged. We have, instead, begun to understand that what we once thought were ordered sequences or steps are better understood as additions to a growing repertoire. Drawing development provides a prime example as well as a powerful way in which to understand the significance of this change of paradigm. Nearly 20 years ago, through her intensive observations of children drawing, Nancy Smith—

whose work is at the root of this book—argued that by the age of 4 or 5, young children have already developed a number of different drawing systems, picking and choosing which to use when. In this way, they are much like mature artists. In fact, a 5-year-old can make articulate choices about which of several developing idioms she or he wants to use—the stylized indications of maps and diagrams, the selective shapes of schematic or memory-based drawing, or the visually detailed alertness of close observational drawing.

So, courtesy of these teacher-researchers, we have a fresh image set of developmental assumptions to replace those that informed Luquet. Different from what familiar stage theory would predict, these varied systems do not necessarily atrophy once more realistic drawing systems emerge. Given a social and functional niche, these multiple graphic languages can mature (Matthews, 1984; Smith & Fucigna, 1988; Wolf & Perry, 1988). In place of an ascending stair of orderly stages, what results is a wide repertoire of choices—very much like Darwin's branching coral. This, in turn, suggests quite a different conception of sophistication or end-points. Rather than moving steadily towards only the mastery of the finer points of realism, children are building a repertoire of systems or strategies for visual meaning-making. The acme is not, "Can I show the receding side of the house?" but rather "When do I render that house as a dot; as a thick, enclosing circle; in spare cross-section; or in detailed perspective?" The answer is that it depends on whether those marks are to be part of a map, a poster to collect aid for refugees, a portrait of a house for a real estate ad, or an elevation drawing for engineers. If Sir Isaac Newton were to come up with an image for this expanded notion of drawing development, it might well be the color spectrum. If Frida Kahlo were to draw it, it would be an eye from which grew many graceful arms, with each hand tracing a different image, each a distinct response to the same chair or dog.

While this enlarged view of drawing development clearly has many implications for theory and research, it also speaks to teaching. In this revised view of drawing development, which graphic languages emerge is no longer dictated by the iron hand of developmental stages. Instead, it is much more likely to be the result of the liveliness and diversity of the visual cultures in which children grow up. Young children can make diagrams and tallies, they can construct simple maps, they can draw from memory or from observation. They can also cartoon and illustrate (Wilson & Wilson, 1977). But the stunning point that the chapters in this book drive home is this: The eye's many tongues flourish only where they are recognized and nurtured. For years, 5-, 6-, 7-, and 8-year-olds drew only from memory—not because they couldn't grapple with the spokes of bicycles or the receding wing of a huge stuffed bird, but because they were never invited to try and never helped to learn how. In essence, development and its directions are less in data and more in the eye of the beholder (Pariser, 1995). Thin expectations yield thin opportunities, which, in turn, yield thin performance.

Thus the work of the teachers and children in this volume argues forcibly for a radically different conception of drawing development and for a much more active and thoughtful form of teaching. But for something else as well. Quite possibly, the notion of a repertoire of drawing systems is appealing to teacher–researchers working in contemporary classrooms because it comes at a particular moment in our own history. One of the most potent ideas in teaching and human development of the last half century has been that of diversity—a breaking up of an old, even fossilized, notion of one single excellence. In its place, we have a growing understanding of multiple intelligences (Gardner, 1983) as well as the important educational contributions of multi-culturalism. Yet vital as each of these concepts is, both are fundamentally about parallel forms of variety or difference. Neither captures what is fundamentally human—the choosing and juggling of many identities, the essential pluralism of the human imagination.

In many ways, this volume is a reflection on the possibility of such a project, explored from the perspective of teaching children how to draw. Though the teacher-researchers writing here are modest, their work offers us an image of a child whose comic book drawings do not compromise his observational drawings, whose maps do not betray her landscapes. It is an image of multi-lingualism as an endpoint. What is promising—if not yet fully claimed—about this revised account of drawing development is that it uses the lively and irrefutable data of children's drawings to argue that this capacity to shift identities, moving among different communities of culture, language, and usage, is one of the most inventive, and adaptive, aspects of being human. It is especially powerful to have this argument coming from a working group of teacher–researchers. After all, it is they who must have the will and the understanding to create classroom cultures where each child, not different children, thinks and speaks in many languages.

Dennie Palmer Wolf
Harvard Graduate School of Education

REFERENCES

Clark, M. C. (1995). *Children's understanding of genre in drawing: An examination of strategy use in observation and memory drawing by children aged five through eight.* Unpublished doctoral dissertation, Harvard University Graduate School of education, Cambridge, MA.

Danto, A. (1994). *Embodied meanings: Critical essays and aesthetic meditations.* New York: Farrar Straus Giroux.

Freeman, N., & Cox, M. V. (Eds.). (1985). *Visual order: The nature and development of pictorial representation.* Cambridge: Cambridge University Press.

Gardner, H. (1983). *Frames of mind: The theory of multiple intelligences.* New York: Basic Books.

Luquet, G-H. (1913). *Les dessins d'un enfant: Thèse pour le doctorat présenté à la faculté des lettres de l'université de Lille.* Paris: Librarie Felix Alcan.

Matthews, J. (1984). Children drawing: Are young children really scribbling? *Early Child Development and Care, 18,* 1–39.

Pariser, D. (1995). *A cross-cultural examination of the U-curve in aesthetic development.* Spencer Foundation Small Grant Final Report.

Smith, N. R., & Fucigna, C. (1988). Drawing systems in children's pictures: Contour and form. *Visual Arts Research, 14,* 91–95.

Varnedoe, K., & Gopnik, A. (1990). *Modern art and popular culture. Readings in high and low.* New York: Henry N. Abrahms.

Wilson, B., & Wilson, M. (1977). An iconoclastic view of the imagery sources in the drawings of young people. *Art Education, 30*(1), 4–12.

Wolf, D. P., & Perry, M. D. (1988). From endpoints to repertoires: Some new conclusions about drawing development. *Journal of Aesthetic Education, 22,* 17–34.

Preface and Acknowledgments

Nancy Ray Smith was the guiding force behind this book. Her leadership and commitment to children and teaching prompted the formation of the Drawing Study Group.

Since October 1982, we have been meeting regularly to talk about art education. Our primary focus has been observation drawing. Early on in our get-togethers we decided that our discussions, our experiences, and our reflections should result in a book. Our common belief in the value and importance of observation drawing has kept us energized. Now we want to stimulate others to try the approach and techniques we have learned. And we are eager to describe how children fascinate and impress us with their efforts at drawing from observation.

Nancy Smith died in June 1990. We commend to you her book *Experience and Art: Teaching Children to Paint* (1983/1993). She explores in it the relationship between theory and practice and explains the connection between child development and art education. Her work is a sturdy base for this one. She discussed with us the format and content of this book and wrote the initial draft of Chapter 1, but the preparation of the rest of the book has been in our hands.

Our work is offered in recognition of Nancy's contributions to the field of art education in general and to the Drawing Study Group in particular. Our hope is that this book will inspire others, as Nancy has each one of us.

We wish to thank the following:

One another and our family members.

Judith Burton, who reviewed the initial draft, made many helpful suggestions, and gave us encouragement.

Susan Liddicoat, of Teachers College Press, who gave gracious support throughout the publication process.

Terri Manchester, who typed many revisions with patient and cheerful expertise.

Fran Watts, who contributed her time and talent to proofreading our final draft of the manuscript.

We especially want to thank each child who whether mentioned or not has added to our appreciation of observation drawing.

Laraine Cicchetti	Barbara Gordon-O'Connor
Margaret C. Clark	Barbara A. Halley
Carolee Fucigna	Margaret Kennedy

Observation Drawing with Children
A Framework for Teachers

one

What Is Drawing?

The act of drawing has different outcomes for both adults and children, depending on the artist's intention. There are maps, diagrams, and plans made primarily for practical purposes. There are images of imaginary beings and places, as in Sir John Tenniel's drawings for *Alice in Wonderland* (Figure 1.1a) or a 7-year-old's picture of planes bombing dinosaurs and volcanoes (Figure 1.1b).

There are renderings of the expressive essence of objects, as in Matisse's drawings of the round voluptuousness of women (Figure 1.2a) or a 9-year-old's rendering of a fat, curvy rabbit (Figure 1.2b).

There are schematized renderings of objects in narrative pictures, as in ancient Egyptian wall paintings (Figure 1.3a) or a 7-year-old's drawing of her sister sleepwalking at night (Figure 1.3b).

And there are images offering the illusion of a visual experience, as in the nature studies of Dürer (Figure 1.4a) or an 11-year-old's rendering of her boot (Figure 1.4b).

This short list—practical, imaginary, expressive, schematic, narrative, and illusory—includes only some of the most common intentions that motivate drawing.

Note that illusionism—that is, the representation of the world from a single, static viewpoint, sometimes achieved through the use of techniques such as perspective—is the artist's intention in only one kind of drawing. Most people think that the primary purpose of drawing is to create a visual

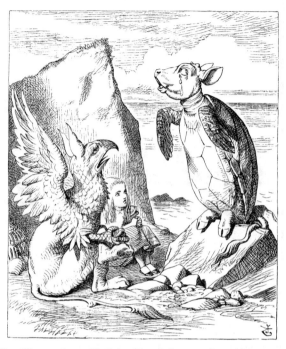

FIG. 1.1A: Alice Illustration, Sir John Tenniel, reproduced by arrangement with Macmillan Children's Books.

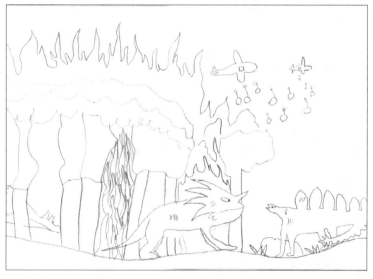

FIG. 1.1B: *Dinosaurs, Volcanoes, and Bombs*, Grade Two.

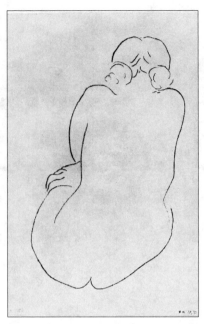

FIG. 1.2A: *Seated Nude, Back Turned* {Nu assis, vu de dos}, Henri Mattisse (1913); Lithograph, printed in black, composition: 16 5/8" x 10 3/8" (42.3 cm x 26.4 cm); The Museum of Modern Art, New York.
Gift of Mrs. John D. Rockefeller, 3rd.; Photograph © 1998 The Museum of Modern Art, New York; Copyright © 1997 Succession H. Matisse, Paris/Artists Rights Society (ARS) New York.

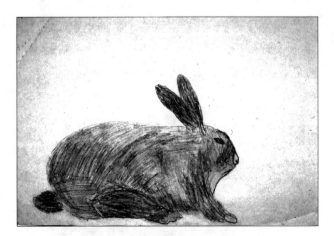

FIG. 1.2B: *Fat Curvy Rabbit,* Grade Three.

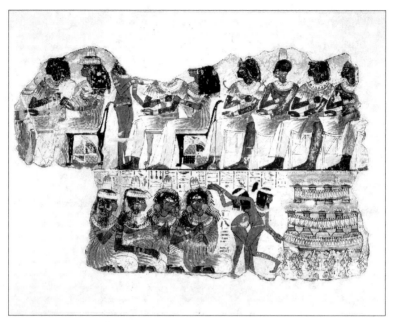

FIG. 1.3A: Banqueting Scene. Wall painting from Neb-Amun's Tomb at Thebes, c. 1370 B.C. Copyright British Museum.

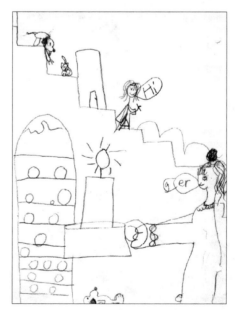

FIG. 1.3B: My Sister Sleepwalking, Grade Two.

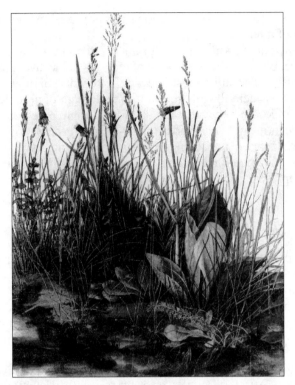

FIG. 1.4A: The Great Piece of Turf, Albrecht Dürer, 1503, courtesy of Graphische Sammlung Albertina, Wien.

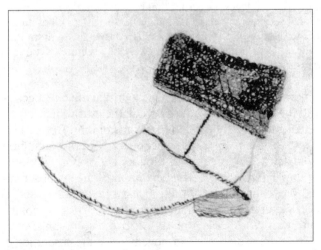

FIG. 1.4B: Boot, Josie Ann, Grade Five.

illusion. They also believe that illusionism is achieved by making an accurate replica of a retinal image.

As trained artists know, it is not possible to make an exact replica of a retinal image, because the perception of reality is subjective. First, the artist must select the information most relevant for the kind of drawing intended. Information considered highly relevant to a diagram of an object could be considered irrelevant if the artist is responding to light on an object. Second, because objects are not delimited by marks as much as by surfaces, the artist must devise a means of translating those surfaces into marks on paper. Finally, since we live in three-dimensional space, the artist must use or invent a system to represent depth and volume on a flat sheet of paper.

DEFINING OBSERVATION DRAWING

In many of the kinds of drawing mentioned above, children or adults work from memory or imagination. But sometimes, they draw from observation. Observation drawing is especially subject to the assumption that its purpose is visual illusionism—an assumption we challenge. Instead, we propose that the intent of observation drawing is the creation of what the artist Nathan Goldstein (1977) describes as a "responsive" drawing.

> All drawings motivated by a wish to inquire and to experience . . . are *responsive*. They are all founded on our intellectual and intuitive judgments about a subject and its organized expression on the page. . . .
> Here *responsive* refers to our perceptual, aesthetic, and empathetic interpretations of a subject's properties that hold potential for creative drawing. In responsive drawing, comprehending a subject's actualities precedes and affects the quality of our responses. Such drawings do more than recall what our outer or inner world looks like. They tell us what our intuitive knowledge informs us it is. (p. 11)

Observation drawing can be defined as responsive drawing because it helps the artist and the viewer to become aware of the elusive as well as the obvious qualities of subjects. It helps, in the words of John Dewey (1934/1958), to "concentrate" and "enlarge" our experience. With this definition in mind, it becomes easier to comprehend a broader set of possible intentions for observation drawing that move well beyond illusionism. Observation drawing, for example, can be part of the process of learning to see. And thus, the marks on paper are tracks that record the process of looking, not the presentation of an illusion (Figure 1.5). It can also be an investigation of the internal structure of an object, its movement, or the proportion of its forms (Figure 1.6).

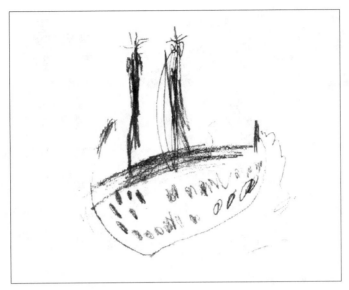

FIG. 1.5: Narcissi, Michael, Kindergarten.

Observation drawing can entail responding to the expressivity of an object or imagining one's personal vision of an object (Figure 1.7). Representation, then, is secondary to emotion.

Finally, an observation drawing can be an exploration of artistic issues held important to the artist. These may be understood by the viewer as the artist understood them, or they may be understood in a mode specific to the viewer. For example, a Michelangelo study for the Sistine ceiling carried different meaning for a Roman of his time than it carries for a contemporary viewer. In another instance, a 7-year-old's figure drawing carries sufficient information for her, but not for many adults.

MEANING AND AESTHETICS IN OBSERVATION DRAWING

Observation drawings can convey meaning to the viewer in three ways. The most familiar is the narrative, the story of the subject depicted. Drawings such as Rembrandt's *Saskia Asleep in Bed* or *My New Bicycle* exemplify meaning conveyed through narrative (Figures 1.8a and b).

Almost as familiar is the metaphor. In these observation drawings, the objects depicted stand for ideas or emotions. For example, Dürer's *Hands in Adoration* implies the experience of religious worship; an 11-year-old's *Weeping Tree* suggests the child's growing sense of human loneliness and isolation (Figures 1.9a and b).

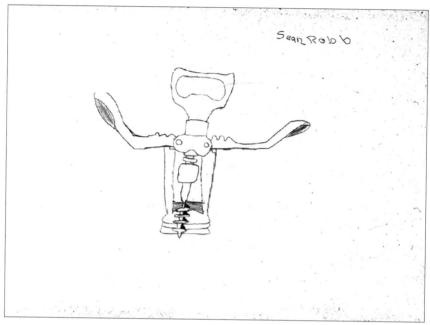

FIG. 1.6: *Corkscrew*, Sean, Grade Four.

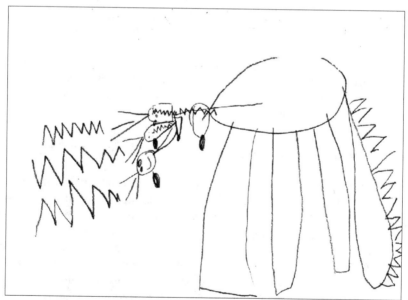

FIG. 1.7: *Dragon*, Devra, Kindergarten.

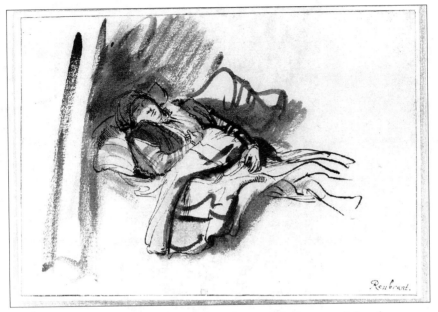

FIG. 1.8A: Saskia Asleep in Bed, Rembrandt, c. 1635. Courtesy Ashmolean Museum, Oxford.

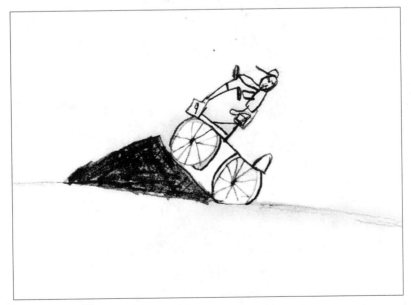

FIG. 1.8B: My New Bicycle, Grade Three.

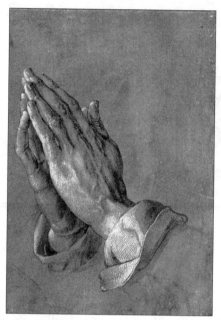

FIG. 1.9A: *Hands in Adoration*, by Albrecht Dürer, courtesy of Graphische Sammlung Albertina, Vienna.

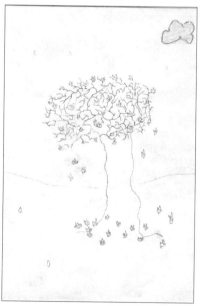

FIG. 1.9B: *Weeping Tree*, Grade Five.

Finally, there is the expressive mode of conveying meaning. This mode ranges from the emotional character of the composition and forms, such as the *Weeping Tree* and *The Dragon* (Figure 1.7), to the meaning in marks. Depending on the arrangement of lines, shapes, and values (lightness and darkness) in a composition, an object or scene can be made to appear tranquil or agitated, eerie or exuberant.

The ability to see meaning in marks is a phenomenon of perception that causes the viewer to sense such things as motion in a flowing line even though it is lying fixed and still, or weight and balance in groups of shapes even though they are merely an arrangement of lines on flat paper. The artist's convincing and sensitive deployment of meaning in the marks used in a picture creates the difference between mundane drawing and one that evokes excitement and insight in the viewer.

It might seem that expressive properties in drawings are phenomena too remote for children to understand and use. Nonetheless, response to expressive properties is a primary mode of perception for young children; in fact, it is probably the basis of the aesthetic aspect of their drawing (Smith, 1979, 1987). The insightful developmental psychologist Heinz Werner (1957/1978) describes this sort of perception as a primordial manner of perceiving and states that "it grows in certain individuals such as artists, to a level not below but on par with that of 'geometric-technical' perception and logical discourse" (p. 123).

When drawing from observation, the child applies expressive perception to looking at objects and to making marks on paper. The child first directs his perception toward an object, searching for characteristics such as the movement of its forms and structures, and then tries to establish similar characteristics in the marks of the drawing. This process is repeated as the drawing develops (Arnheim, 1974; Smith, 1983).

Thus the ability to perceive expressive properties and produce organized records of their responses is well within the reach of children. In fact, these abilities go through developmental changes that have been described in the work of Biber (1936/1962), Willats (1977a, 1981), Burton (1980–1981), Smith and Fucigna (1988), and Clark (1995). Conscious use of the three modes of conveying meaning emerge in a particular developmental pattern beginning with narrative and followed by expressive and then metaphoric meaning (Smith, 1990). This development generally occurs when opportunities to draw from observation are combined with thoughtful interactions between children, teachers, and peers. Art education that focuses on observation drawing concretizes strategies children have been using unconsciously and furthers their understanding that this kind of responsive drawing is not a matter of talent but a matter of hard work and thinking.

ATTITUDES TOWARD OBSERVATION DRAWING IN ART EDUCATION

Although research and practice have shown that children have the capacity for expressive perception and the ability to produce organized and expressive records of their responses, observation drawing has been misunderstood or absent from art curricula in the United States. Sometimes U.S. children are encouraged to use observation drawing to record information in science and social studies, but not in art. Some U.S. art teachers seem to feel that young children cannot draw from observation, and should not be asked to do so, because observation drawing might undermine children's natural abilities and creativity (Clark, 1995). This attitude has multiple historical roots.

The ancient Greeks saw drawing as scientific inquiry (Gombrich, 1969). The skilled artist's objective was to create an illusion so believable that the viewer would be deceived. This view of drawing faded by the Middle Ages but reemerged when Alberti developed the drawing system of perspective during the early Renaissance. The use of perspective to create an illusion of depth and space remains a favored method of spatial representation in Westernized art today. Drawings that do not create this believable illusion, such as those created by children, are sometimes criticized as inaccurate or as failed attempts at realism (Clark, 1897).

Researchers involved in some of the early studies of the psychology of children's art also judged children's drawings by illusionistic criteria. Luquet (1927), believing that children base their work on knowledge rather than perceptual information, suggests that children draw what they know and not what they see. Lowenfeld and Brittain (1982), in their influential textbook on art education, describe children's drawings as "schematic" or "generalized." Piaget and Inhelder (1948, 1969) noted that young children tend to include all of the salient features of an item whether they are visible or not.

The growth of nonrepresentational art in this country, which began with the Armory Show of 1913 in New York City, may have been another influential factor in the underutilization of observation drawing in U.S. art classes. Artists such as Grant Wood and John Stuart Curry turned away from the regional realism that until then had characterized art in this country and began to emphasize free expression. This shift finally culminated in the abstract expressionist movement of the 1950s.

While tradition and research argued that children could not draw from observation, progressive forces in art education neglected observation drawing in the literature. Children's work was believed to evolve naturally toward more adult forms (Kellogg, 1970). Attempts to guide or influence that evolution were seen as potentially damaging (Schaefer-Simmern,

1961). Art educators believed that noninterventive methods supported children's natural ways of working with art materials. Thus, children's natural work was considered "inaccurate," yet teaching children to draw "accurately" was considered damaging.

Whether all or some of these factors contributed to a lack of consistency in the teaching of observation drawing is not clear, but the fact remains that observation drawing has been either omitted or misunderstood in public school art curricula.

This book questions some of these long-standing assumptions about observation drawing and presents new, more constructive ways for it to be included in elementary art curricula. Modernism has shown us that illusionism is just one of the many systems available for the creation of viable representation. Recent research indicates that children seek out opportunities to draw from observation (Clark, 1989); that children use drawing as a problem-solving activity requiring cognitive, perceptual, and technical skills (Golomb, 1992); that children discover increasingly complex drawing strategies (Willats, 1977a; Colbert & Taunton, 1985; Smith, 1985); and that children select strategies according to the intended purpose of their drawing (Wolf & Perry, 1988; Clark, 1995).

Observation drawing has always been a staple of elementary art curricula in Great Britain and Italy. Great Britain's most recent version of its National Curriculum in Art clearly states the importance of including observation drawing (Thistlewood, 1992). And in the provocative and much-studied curriculum of Reggio Emilia, Italy, children have "extensive experience" with drawing from observation and from imagination (Katz, 1993).

Art teachers in the United States who incorporate observation drawing in a developmentally sensitive context report that children approach it with enthusiasm (Clark, 1989) and provide articulate descriptions of their drawing strategy choices (Burton, 1980–1981; Clark, 1995). The assumption that children cannot and should not draw from observation is questionable in the light of this new information.

CONTEXT AND GOAL OF OBSERVATION DRAWING

We believe that children should be offered many opportunities to draw from observation—opportunities that are consistent with children's intentions and are grounded in a solid understanding of child development. Research conducted by Willats (1977b), Burton (1980), Smith (1983), Smith and Fucigna (1988), and Clark (1995), as well as our own many years of classroom experience, support the notion that observation drawing should not use correct illusionism as its goal. Instead, observation drawing should be guided by the more sophisticated understanding that it is responsive drawing and that it resides in a particular context and has a particular goal.

The context for observation drawing with 4- to 12-year-olds is defined by six principles.

1. Children within this age range are developing a repertoire of drawing strategies for capturing their visual world. Their choice of strategy depends on the intent of their drawing, which might be a map of their route to school or something very different, such as a description of the landmarks they pass.
2. Observation drawing is an intellectual, emotional, and intuitive response to objects and events, not a "correct" rendering or visual illusion.
3. Observation drawing involves the translation of this response into marks on paper.
4. Marks on paper have a meaning of their own, in addition to the objects they depict. A line that represents the edge of a saw is in itself sharp and jagged.
5. Children's responses and translations change with age and education. For example, a 5-year-old's drawing of a three-headed dragon figure may be focused on the number of dragon body parts present, while an 11-year-old's drawing displays a response to the textures on the dragon's body.
6. There are individual differences in responses and translations within a given age group. One 5-year-old may focus on the fact that the dragon has three heads, while another may focus on the fact that the dragon has many sharp teeth.

The goal of observation drawing for young children is the development of mental and physical abilities used in the discovery and creation of meaning through drawing. This book offers teachers guidance in helping children reach that goal.

two

Teaching Children to Draw from Observation

Children are challenged to think as they draw from observation just as they are when they paint, sculpt, or make collages. They think about using art materials and developing strategies for representation. They think about conveying meaning and understanding aesthetic properties.

What is the role of the teacher in presenting observation drawing to children? The teacher's task is not to tell children steps to follow to carry out that cognitive challenge; the task is to enable children to construct their own individual drawing strategies.

The teacher lays the foundation for observation drawing by giving students extensive experience with materials. She builds a framework by keeping in mind developmental guidelines, and by planning lessons with clearly defined objectives and in carefully crafted sequence. She sustains it by choosing objects suitable for the given age group and appropriate to lesson objectives. She bolsters it by fostering aesthetic properties and encouraging awareness of them. Essential to all aspects of that framework are the ways the teacher motivates, guides, and responds to children as they draw. The aim is to stimulate each child's thinking and cultivate it as it grows and changes from month to month, year to year.

This book describes how teachers can provide children with opportunities to do observation drawing. Explicit instructions with predictable outcomes are not included; instead, a specific approach is described through a series of lesson plans focused on children 4 to 12 years old. These plans are organized around four developmental periods: kindergarten, first and second grades, third and fourth grades, and fifth and sixth grades. Each of these developmental periods forms a chapter in the book. Within each chapter there are two main sections: a developmental framework and a set of lesson plans. In this chapter we provide an explanation of those sections.

DEVELOPMENTAL FRAMEWORK

To help teachers view children's work in observation drawing within the appropriate developmental framework, each chapter begins with a description of characteristics pertaining to a particular age group. The following topics are included:

1. *General development.* What are children of this age like? What are their cognitive abilities, social concerns, and interests? In all education, knowledge of child development is the bedrock of good teaching practice. In art education, this knowledge helps teachers select objectives for their lessons based on what is important to children during any one particular period.

2. *Representation.* In observation drawing, children must invent strategies to translate what they are looking at onto a flat sheet of paper. These strategies are based on three vital components: what the child understands about the object being drawn, what the child understands about the materials being used to create the drawing, and how the child makes correspondences between the materials and the object being observed. Choice of strategies is influenced by experiential history, art education, individual differences, culture, and development. What kinds of strategies do children invent for representation during the four developmental periods?

3. *Aesthetics.* Aesthetic properties emerge in drawing when a correspondence is made between the expressive qualities of an object and the expressive qualities of a material. For example, the sharp, poking, zigzag line used by a child to show the scales of an iguana is considered aesthetic because a connection has been made between the way the child experiences the feeling of the scales and the way the pencil has been manipulated to show them. The object itself is not defined as aesthetic. The drawing gains aesthetic properties through the child's creation and use of variation in marks, lines and shapes.

    The ability to perceive the expressive qualities inherent in objects, experiences, and materials relies on a particular type of perception defined by Heinz Werner (1957/1978) as "physiognomic." Motoric and sensory phenomena are used in forming concepts, as are qualities of affectivity, expressivity, and energy (Smith, 1987). As quoted in Chapter 1, "response to expressive properties is a primary mode of perception for young children, in fact, it is probably the basis of the aesthetic aspect of their drawing." Very early in their development they begin to compose, select, and arrange graphic elements. This creates aesthetic order and interest in their drawings (Smith, 1983).

In Chapters 3–6, children's developmental stages in aesthetics are defined by their level of awareness of the aesthetic properties within their own drawings and the drawings of their peers, and by their control of aesthetic properties within their own work. This aesthetic understanding is significantly influenced by education. Education that offers formulas strips children's drawings of their life, energy, and integrity. But reinforcing children's own aesthetic ideas strongly affects their awareness and control of these properties. It also prepares them to make aesthetic assessments of adult work later on. With this in mind, we can ask, what are children aware of and in control of in terms of aesthetics during these developmental periods?

4. *Concepts of the material.* Creating a drawing requires translating a person's ideas into the language of drawing materials. The elements of that language are acquired by manipulating tools and materials, including paper, pencils, erasers, and charcoal. As children use these, they begin to form concepts of the material; that is, they begin to form an understanding of the various effects that can be produced. Pencils (#2 or softer) can be used to make dark and light marks, thick and thin lines. Charcoal can make smudgy or sharp lines. Children's concepts of a material evolve when they have frequent opportunities to use that material, whether it be a pencil, a brush, clay, or collage. These concepts vary from person to person because of individual differences, amount of experience with materials, and amount of art education received (Cicchetti, 1991). How do children in the different age groups understand drawing materials: their qualities, their characteristics, or their potential for capturing experience?

5. *Objects to draw.* Selecting an object to draw from observation is a difficult task. It requires matching an actual object to an educational objective, a material, and the interests and skills of a particular age group. This section in Chapters 3–6 provides general guidelines and specific examples for selecting objects that will attract chil-

dren in the given age group. How does the teacher select objects matched to particular lesson objectives and materials?

6. *Problems and responses.* Each chapter describes common problems children face when doing observation drawing and includes responses for dealing with these problems. Children are eager to have adults comment on what they are doing. A teacher's comments can encourage and validate each child's efforts. A quick, "Oh that's good," or "I like it!" does not suffice, because it implies that it is the child's job to please the adult. Value judgments, though difficult to avoid, leave children guessing about how and why their work is "good" and do not provide any specific or helpful feedback. Sensitive responses should highlight the features the child is responding to in the object. The teacher needs to view the drawing through the child's intentions and not as an incomplete or inaccurate representation of the object. What kinds of problems are typical at each age? What kinds of teacher responses are appropriate?

All of these developmental descriptions (overall development, representation, aesthetics, concepts of the material, objects to draw, problems and responses) serve two purposes. If one reads them *across* chapters, one can begin to grasp the context within which observation drawing takes place—how drawings, in general, change with age. If one concentrates, instead, on a single chapter, one can begin to grasp the range of individual responses that can exist *within* a given age group.

LESSON PLANS: IDEAS AND METHODS

In Chapters 3–6 the developmental framework is followed by lesson plans appropriate for each particular age group. These lesson plans provide sample ideas to use with children. More important, they present an approach to working with children when teaching them how to draw from observation. This approach involves several steps ranging from the establishment of an objective for what is to be learned to the evaluation of the drawings produced. Samples of drawings associated with the lesson plans are included in each chapter. These drawings have been selected as examples of the range of products a teacher might expect to see. All are valid responses to the task, reflecting the children's different methods of translating visual information into a drawing on paper.

Every teacher and group of children brings a different set of skills, values, responses, and interests to the challenge of observation drawing. No two classroom situations are alike and children generally thrive in an atmosphere that is flexible and adaptive to their individual interests. It is our hope that these lesson plans will stimulate thinking about how best to integrate observation drawing into one's particular classroom situation.

Establishing Objectives

In developing a lesson plan, one must begin by stating an objective. This is critical, because it establishes what the teacher hopes the children will accomplish through the observation-drawing experience. Four general objectives are presented in this book.

1. *Learning to look.* Learning to look at an object and to reflect on what you see in a new or different way is the first step in all observation drawing. When very young children first attempt observation drawing, learning to look is their major concern. It is, therefore, the primary objective when planning lessons for this age group. For older children, learning to look is the foundation on which they build solutions to more complex drawing problems, such as rendering pattern and texture.
2. *Expression.* Lessons devoted to expression focus on the arrangement and quality of visual elements (line, shape, or texture) as they are used to create an emotional response in the artist and in the viewer. As a way to convey meaning consciously, expression is an appropriate objective for children in third grade and older.
3. *Composition.* Lessons in composition encourage children to think about where they place items on the paper. Relationships between objects themselves and between objects and the paper's edge are emphasized. Lessons dealing with these relationships are appropriate for children in fourth grade and older. Some sixth graders and older children may produce metaphoric meaning in their use of composition. For example, an isolated figure in the paper space may convey loneliness.
4. *Space.* Lessons devoted to spatial issues involve representing the three dimensions of an object or the depth of a space within the two dimensions of the paper. With younger children, the emphasis is on how appearances change according to one's point of view. For older children it means discovering strategies for representing depth and volume.

Guiding Development of Drawing Strategies

Creating or inventing a personal graphic response to some scene or object from nature poses formidable challenges. Children must learn how to look carefully at objects and then develop strategies for translating their observations into marks on paper. The method described here underscores the importance of a teacher's guidance while children are developing personal drawing strategies. This means asking relevant questions when speaking with individuals or when moderating a discussion about drawings with students in the class. The construction of relevant questions requires both a knowledge of drawing development and an appropriate lesson objective. This guidance, in contrast to specific "how-to" directions, helps children acquire confidence in their abilities to tackle this unique graphic problem and highlights the learning that is taking place within each lesson.

Appropriate guidance in the development of strategies for representing space and volume is particularly important in observation drawing. Young children often begin with very concrete strategies for representing front and back. One 5-year-old represents her cat's face on the front of the page and his tail on the back of the page. Another 6-year-old makes a red ball "round and fat" by making multiple layers of red marks within a circular shape (Wolf & Fucigna, 1981). By third or fourth grade, children employ strategies such as overlapping and size-distance scaling to represent in front of and behind or near and far. By sixth grade, most children are trying to figure out more culturally recognizable ways to represent spatial depth and volume.

In our experience, teachers often respond to children's interest in spatial representation by providing adult solutions such as one-point perspective, cross-hatching, or "shading." When children use strategies that they have not developed themselves, their drawings appear contrived and mechanical. Adult artists do not use these strategies in prescribed situations but see them instead as choices in a repertoire they have developed. Maturity is required when attempting to integrate these strategies in a way that genuinely reflects a personal response.

Although it might seem easier to provide some automatic answers to questions of translation, the teacher's role is to ask questions that help children discover their own strategies. Once developed, these strategies will be infinitely more accessible and useful to children.

Format of the Lesson Plans

The lesson plans in Chapters 3–6 will be presented in the following format:

Objective
Materials
Room Arrangement
Motivational Dialogue
    Topic Question
    Association
    Visualization
    Transition
    Sharing and Reflecting
Evaluation
Extensions

Each component of a lesson plan is described below, with an example from the lesson on drawing a tricycle in Chapter 4.

Objective: What will children learn through this drawing experience?

> *Example:* Learning to look. To learn that the parts of a tricycle connect and can be translated into connecting shapes on paper.

Materials: What materials are needed to do the task?

> *Example:* 12" x 18" drawing paper and pencils.

Room Arrangement: A simple physical setup that best facilitates observation drawing is suggested. It is understood that parents, teachers, and children work under many different conditions and constraints with the result that many individual adaptations will be necessary.

> *Example:* Children are seated in a circle around a tricycle. Their work tables are behind them.

Motivational Dialogue: The objective structures the dialogue or motivation that takes place before the children begin to draw. The motivation is what the teacher talks about or does to stimulate reflection. The lesson plans in this book include sample questions and comments of a teacher (identified as "T") and sample responses of children ("C"). Of course, these dialogues always vary from child to child and group to group. (Sample responses of children are not provided in the lesson below.) The challenge of the motivation is to translate the abstract objective into an idea children can understand.

TOPIC QUESTION: Motivations usually begin with a topic question that focuses the children and allows the teacher to find out what they know about a particular object or subject. All lesson plans in this book provide sample topic questions. Some include examples of children's verbal responses. The responses chosen display great diversity, but all can be considered age appropriate.

> *Example:* Who remembers using this kind of bike when you were little? What is this kind of bike called?

ASSOCIATION: Through dialogue, the teacher helps the children to clarify their ideas and build enthusiasm for the topic being considered. During the association period, the teacher should be prepared with relevant questions to keep the dialogue going.

> *Example:* How are the wheels the same and different? Who can tell me why this trike has two small wheels in the back? Which parts help you steer?

VISUALIZATION: The visualization period is a critical juncture. During this time the teacher poses questions to help students figure out how to translate their responses to the object into marks and lines on the paper. Visualization questions should continue to focus the children on the objective of the lesson and, more important, encourage the children to think of their *own* strategies for translation into the material.

Visualizations should not provide teacher-generated solutions to the drawing problems at hand. In fact, when children listen to peers, they often receive many more pertinent solutions to the challenges they are facing.

> *Example:* Which parts are connected to the big wheel and how will you draw their shapes? How will you draw the handlebars?

TRANSITION: Finally, in the transition period, the teacher helps the children begin drawing by posing questions about where to start their picture.

> *Example:* Which part of the trike will you draw first? Which part of the trike will you draw next and how will you connect it to the first part?

SHARING AND REFLECTING: The purpose of these questions is to point out what children did and to help them notice particular qualities or strategies evident in their drawings. It is important for children to spend time examining their work together at the end of each lesson. Children often learn from one another, especially if the teacher is careful to point out the specific strategies each of them has used to represent the object. Various aspects of the drawings should be discussed in terms appropriate to the group. Through this process the teacher can re-emphasize the overall objective of the lesson, as well as reveal and support each student's imaginative interpretation and aesthetic response. Dialogue about children's work can occur between teacher and child, teacher and group, or between child and child.

Time needs to be scheduled for this kind of discussion. For very young children, the most productive time is immediately after a drawing session. The best method is to pin up work on the wall so all the work is clearly visible to each child. Another way to share is for children to sit in a circle and hold their work or place it on the floor in front of them.

Having children take the time to describe their own work and the work of others helps sharpen skills of observation and communication. Learning to look closely at each other's work helps them reflect on their efforts. This kind of sharing and reflecting brings to consciousness the processes used in making a drawing, thus emphasizing the thinking involved. Being aware of his own strategies shows a child that drawing is a matter of looking and thinking, not a matter of luck or special talent, factors that are beyond his control. Clarifying what a child already knows and what she has done gives her strategies she can use and depend on in her next drawing (Halley, 1991).

> *Example:* What shapes did Rebecca draw to show the wheels of the trike? Which wheel is biggest? How did Jessie show that the front wheel connects to the handlebars?

Evaluation: The concluding evaluation questions are for teachers to ask themselves in order to determine the effectiveness of the lesson. Was the objective right for the age group? Did the object fit the objective? Did the visualization questions really emphasize the objective?

> *Example:* Have the children paid attention to the parts of the trike and translated them into shapes in their drawings? Have they shown how these shapes are connected?

Evaluation serves another purpose as well. It helps the teacher determine where to go next in planning a future sequence of lessons in observation drawing.

The point of sequencing by complexity is to help children become more confident through a deeper understanding of the subject matter and a deeper understanding of the materials used to represent that subject. The lessons in each chapter are arranged, in general, in order of difficulty. Individual teachers need to determine what might be an appropriate next experience for a particular group. Sequencing is based on the results of each lesson and the interests, struggles, and abilities of the group. For example, if children are very interested in vehicles, they could draw toy cars and trucks. If students need more practice in observing connecting parts, they could draw playground equipment.

Extensions: Extensions are suggestions for further experiences found at the end of each lesson. They extend children's thinking about a particular objective or object and often involve the use of other media such as clay, paint, or collage materials, each of which has unique qualities and limitations. While the focus of this book is drawing, these different materials may be used when working from observation as long as the children have had prior and extensive experience using them.

> *Example:* Children could continue to explore how parts connect by drawing simple mechanical objects. They could create a three-dimensional construction in which one or more of the connected parts can move. Making a collage of the tricycle would help children focus on the quality of the trike's shapes.

The challenges confronting the teacher trying the approach and techniques described in this book are as great as those facing each child drawing from observation. The teacher must carry out rigorous preparation for each drawing experience, pay careful attention to each experience while it happens, and engage in continual reflection and evaluation. The job is demanding, exciting, and rewarding.

three | *Kindergarten*

DEVELOPMENTAL FRAMEWORK

Birthdays, friends, and bad guys—these are but a few of the concerns that take on increasing significance for 4- and 5-year-olds. The world of me, myself, and I expands to include others. To find out about this world of self and beyond, young children seek active experiences with materials and equipment. They need opportunities to experiment with and explore ideas, feelings, and relationships. Most 4- and 5-year-olds are eager to master a wide range of skills; from riding a bike to fitting together a puzzle, from using a hammer or paintbrush to finding a playmate to do "pirates" or "wild dogs." During most of this stage of development, fantasy and reality remain blended; the large stick discovered in the sandbox is labeled a dinosaur bone, the cracker crumbled into many pieces creates a bigger snack.

Vivid and valuable experiences in learning can occur for children in the kindergarten classroom when their characteristics and interests are acknowledged. When planning art curricula, it is essential that the teacher keep in mind these developmental characteristics in general, and artistic ones in particular.

Representation

Most 4- and 5-year-old children have developed a knowledge of lines and shapes and are finding ways to configure marks to represent their ideas. This knowledge is necessary for drawing from observation. The ability to make representations, whether from memory or from observation, evolves at an earlier age through discoveries about lines, shapes, and the space of the paper. Knowing how children make these discoveries is critical to understanding children's development in observation drawing.

The first of these earlier discoveries is that motions made with a tool on a surface leave marks. Next, children find that they can control their motions to make desired marks. These controlled marks become lines. These lines have direction and length and can be straight or curved. Since lines are the result of a motion, children can characterize them as slow, fast, bold, or gentle.

When it touches itself, a line makes a shape. This discovery leads children to consider the inside and the outside area of shapes. The understanding of inside and outside provides children with different places to put other lines and shapes; that is, inside, outside, or on the edge of a shape. These configurations may be considered designs or representations by the child. They can stand for things or experiences in the child's world. The child notices the relationship between the simple attributes of the drawn configuration and those of the object or experience named. For example, a circle with marks inside and lines perpendicular to the edge could be a person or an animal. The very young child will look at what is drawn and then decide what he has made; the older child will decide what to make and then make it (Smith et al., 1983/1993). When that ability to predetermine what to draw occurs, drawing from observation can be introduced.

In observation drawing, young children use specific strategies based on their earlier discoveries about lines, shapes, and arrangements (Smith et al., 1983/1993). One can identify use of the following three strategies:

1. Reducing what is seen into basic or simple shapes, circles, triangles, and squares. Figure 3.4a shows the back view of a dragon drawn using basic shapes.
2. Noticing all the parts, how many there are, and showing their number in relation to the whole. Figure 3.3a is a playground structure in which lines and shapes stand for the different kinds of parts, their numerosity and their relation to the whole.
3. Recording what is seen by following the edge or the contour of the object. In Figure 3.4b, the side view of a dragon, long, curving lines reveal the necks, back, and tail.

Children use a strategy based on the nature of the object being drawn or the particular view from which they see the object. For example, a child can see the curves of the dragon most easily from the side view, and so she uses Strategy 3. But the curves of the same dragon are not as visible from the back view, and so a child chooses Strategy 1. In another instance, a child may respond to a particular characteristic of the object. For example, the child who drew the climbing structure in Figure 3.3a seemed intrigued with the numerous cross pieces, supports, and rings that make up the structure's whole and thus used Strategy 2.

Children of this age may not realize which strategy they are using, or even be aware that they are using a strategy. Some children are more comfortable using only one strategy for all kinds of objects. Recognition of the three strategies described here will help the teacher plan appropriate lesson objectives and choose objects to match those objectives. The teacher can help children decide which strategy they might use by discussing the possibilities in the opening dialogue.

Aesthetics

An observation drawing by a 4- or 5-year-old is really a response to the object. At this age, the aesthetic aspect is not the result of a conscious effort. Instead, it is the result of the way children do mark-making, that is, through motion (Smith et al., 1983/1993). A child moves his pencil around the paper in various directions and speeds and might make car noises as he works. The result is a line that records those fast, curvy, or slow, straight movements. The child may also announce that he has made a racing car. The pleasure the child derives from controlling the speed and pressure of the pencil on the paper's surface gives the line its expressive qualities. Young children do not differentiate between the expressive qualities of the object and its literal form.

When children draw from observation, they are responding to an object and recording their response to it rather than making a faithful copy of it. The response is based either on previous experience with the object or on a first impression of something never seen before. Nevertheless, in the process of making the drawings, children will try to relate what they note to be important qualities of the object to what they know about making different kinds of marks, lines, and shapes.

Children recognize that lines they make can be fast, bold, slow, or gentle; they also sense that shapes can be little or large, light or heavy. They discover that edges can be made sharp, smooth, rough, or bumpy.

In the drawing process, children naturally strive for some kind of resolution or order that gives a feeling of unity to the drawing. This sense of order enables them to arrange marks, lines, and shapes in ways that vary and repeat. Five-year-olds are capable of recognizing where lines or shapes are the same or different in their drawings.

Brenda's drawing of the three-headed dragon (Figure 3.4b) has variety, expressivity, and unity. She repeats the same curved shape for each neck.

She enlarges the three necks and places the second and third ones farther away from the body. She makes the third neck very thick and long, and in response to its apparent weight, she attaches one of the dragon's legs underneath it for support. The dragon's tail is similar in shape and size to the largest neck but is curved in the opposite direction. It swoops down and under the body instead of out and up. The tail also forms a support for the dragon's large body. She arranges her lines and shapes using repetition and variation in a simple but effective manner to convey both movement and balance. These are aesthetic properties in Brenda's drawing.

It is important to help children notice the aesthetic qualities of their work. Noticing these qualities encourages them to use them more consciously and to consider them integral aspects of the drawing process. In examining children's observation drawings for aesthetic use of line, shape, and texture, we find that 4- and 5-year-olds rarely use texture unless the object demands attention to that feature in some way. For example, Brenda shows the scales by adding very short, close-together lines to the end of the dragon's tail and the beginning of his body.

Concepts of the Material

Young children find tools and materials intriguing, and they naturally explore and experiment with them when given the opportunity. They need lots of time to learn how to manipulate various art materials before they can use them confidently. For example, they need to find out about the simple mechanics and properties of pencils, erasers, paper, and paint. Given many opportunities to use these tools and materials, children develop awareness of what can be done with them. Whenever children experience a period without access to particular materials, they must be given time to become reacquainted with them.

Once they are familiar with some of the potential mark-making possibilities of pencils, children can be introduced to observation drawing. An observation drawing experience with 4- and 5-year-olds will run more smoothly if the teacher provides ample supplies and easy access to them. Careful and complete preparations avoid distractions such as those caused by the need to use the pencil sharpener or the conflicts aroused by obvious differences (that is, pencils of varied sizes and colors). Distractions like these interfere with children's ability to concentrate on the drawing task.

Objects to Draw

Because observation drawing is responsive, the meaning of the object for the child is important to consider. The object must come from within the child's realm of fantasy or reality. It can come from home or school; it can highlight an already existing interest, fear, or query. The personal significance of the object makes it most captivating; for example, a favorite stuffed animal or live pet would be particularly interesting to a child of 4 or 5. The three-headed dragon, a sought-after companion in the block area, proved to be an enticing subject for one group. Some objects raise questions that teachers should anticipate; for example, Is that bird dead? Did you kill it? These were the first concerns raised when children were asked to draw a stuffed loon borrowed from the Audubon Society.

When children can handle and manipulate the object, they come to a clearer understanding of it. They examine the parts making up the whole and grow familiar with the curves and contours of a two-wheeler or with the jagged spikes of a plastic monster. The object, however, must not be too intricate or have many parts or pieces. Even size can be seen as an obstacle. When confronted with a two-wheeler to draw, one kindergartner said, "I can't do it. My paper is way too small!"

To help convince the more hesitant child that the task can be done, choose an object with a simple contour, such as a brontosaurus. Or try one with many simple parts having basic shapes, such as a tonka truck. A plastic necklace with heart-shaped beads exemplifies a simple parts-to-whole relationship.

To support those children who still feel reluctant, use the dialogue at the beginning of the drawing experience to provide additional help. Asking what shapes they might use for the body or wheels of a toy wagon helps children focus on basic shapes. Asking what kind of line to use for the neck or tail of a bird helps children focus on contour. Asking where to make lots of lines or circles to show the parts of a climbing structure helps to point out the relationships between those parts and the whole. Such questions enable children to look at and then draw the particular features of an object.

Problems and Responses

Initial observation drawing experiences for children of this age should be voluntary ones. The teacher's interest and presence are often enough to attract and involve them. Their reactions to the task may be surprising, and obstacles inevitably will arise. One or two kindergarten children, for example, may not have developed basic symbols for drawing objects. Their responses to an object may remain grounded in its expressive qualities (e.g., the racing car as a wavy line). Many 4- and 5-year-olds do not include much information in their drawings. Adults may have difficulty understanding them. Teachers, therefore, must respond and question with care in order to gain a better understanding.

Descriptive comments about the characteristics of particular lines encourage the child to tell more about the drawing. For example, the teacher comments while looking at a drawing of narcissi in Figure 3.2a, "Here you made a very dark line, and over here your lines are all wiggly." The child then replies, "Yes, this is the bowl, and these are the roots." The teacher's descriptive remark acknowledges the child's efforts and confirms the importance of line quality. It also makes the child more aware of the strategy she used and its aesthetic result.

LESSON PLANS

TWO-WHEEL BICYCLE

Several children had been showing great interest and persistence in learning to ride the two-wheel bicycle available to them on the playground. This was chosen as an object to draw.

Objective: Learning to Look: To learn to look at an often-used and well-loved object, to identify its parts and the lines and shapes that make up those parts, and to organize them as a whole in a drawing of a bike.

Materials: 12" x 18" white drawing paper, pencils, and erasers.

Room Arrangement: Children seated at desks facing the side view of a two-wheeler placed on a low table.

Motivational Dialogue

TOPIC QUESTION:
> T: Usually you use this bike outside. Why do you think I've brought it into the classroom?
> C: Are we going to ride it inside?
> C: I want a chance to try.
> C: I need my big brother to help.

ASSOCIATION:
> T: How many of you have ridden this bike outside? Was it hard to ride?
> C: I have, it took a long time to learn.
> T: What part helps you steer?
> C: You sit here and steer here.

VISUALIZATION:

T: I'm going to put the bike on the table so we can see it better.

C: A two-wheeler's gonna sit on a table?

C: Are we going to draw it? No way!

T: Now that it's on the table, what shapes can you see? Where do you see them?

C: A big round shape for the wheel.

C: A little circle here. (The children cluster around the bike pointing out many circles.)

C: There are too many circles. I can't draw this.

T: Well, if there are too many, why don't you start with just one? Which one would you pick?

C: I'd start right around here.

C: I'd make the seat go along like this, come along like that, and then touch up to the handlebars. Then I'd make it come down and touch up to the wheels. (Child touches each part as he describes his plan.)

T: O.K., that's a great plan! Can anybody see some other shapes?

C: I see a square.

C: I see a pear shape, the seat.

C: A bell shape.

T: Show me where you see that shape. (Child points.) Oh, I see, right where the pedal attaches to the wheel. You are really looking carefully. Where would you have to make a curvy line for some parts?

C: Here and here. (Child points to the handle bars.)

T: Are there places where you would make straight lines?

C: Yes, from here to here. (Child points to part connecting handlebars to wheel.)

TRANSITION:

T: You have found a lot of different shapes and lines on the bike. Will you start by making a line or a shape first? Will it be round or some other shape?

C: I'm going to start with the wheel.

C: I'm making the seat shape first.

T: Will you draw a big shape first?

C: My paper is too small.

C: I will have to make it small to fit my paper.

SHARING AND REFLECTING:

T: What are some of the shapes you made in your drawings (Figure 3.1a, b, and c)? Who made some shapes very big and some very

small? Did anyone make parts of the bike very dark? How did
you do that? Show me which drawing has lots of curvy lines.

Evaluation: Were students able to differentiate parts and shapes and then
translate them into shapes and lines in their drawings? Were they able
to connect shapes in ways that correspond to the arrangement of the parts
of the bike?

Extensions: Size is important to children, and they like to do things
together. A group of children could draw an object with many parts, each
child doing one part, and create one very big drawing. They could draw
other large objects using big paper and for contrast draw very small objects
on small paper.

NARCISSI

Objective: Learning to Look: To learn to look at and to translate the
different parts of what is observed into various kinds of lines; that is, curvy
or straight, dark or light, thick or thin.

Materials: 9" x 12" white drawing paper, pencils, erasers, and three nar-
cissus bulbs (sprouted) in a glass bowl with gravel.

Room Arrangement: Six children seated around an oval table with the
bowl of bulbs in the center.

Motivational Dialogue

TOPIC QUESTION:
    T: Who knows what these are?
    C: My grandma has some.
    C: Where are the flowers?

ASSOCIATION:
    T: These plants have different parts. Who can describe them?
    C: There is the brown round part.
    T: Yes. What's that part called?
    C: That's the bulb. It looks like an onion.
    T: Yes, it does. It has some thin loose parts that are like an onion's
        skin. Who can describe another part?

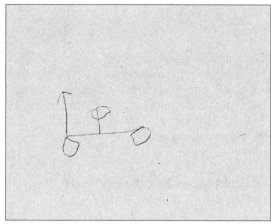

FIG. 3.1A: *Bike*,
Christopher,
Kindergarten.

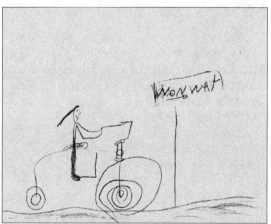

FIG. 3.1B: *Bike*, Carrie,
Kindergarten.

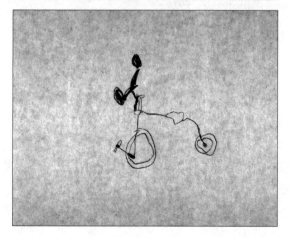

FIG. 3.1C: *Bike*, Mimi,
Kindergarten.

C: There is the long skinny green part.

T: Right! What is that part called?

C: That's the stem.

T: Good. What are some other things we can see?

C: The pebbles and those skinny things mixed in.

T: Yes, that's careful looking. What do you think the skinny things are?

C: They are the roots. We can see them 'cause there's no dirt like in a garden.

T: Yes. These plants grow in water and pebbles.

VISUALIZATION:

T: Now that we have looked very carefully at all the parts, how will you make the shape of the bowl with your pencil?

C: I will make it round.

T: Okay. What kind of pencil marks will you use to show the stem?

C: I will make them fat.

T: Oh, that's a good idea. Show me how you can make your pencil line fat. (Hands a child a pencil and a small piece of paper. The child rubs hard back and forth.) Yes, that's a way to make a line thick and dark. Where might you use light thin lines?

C: For that peeling piece of the round part.

T: Yes, the skin of the bulb is very delicate!

TRANSITION:

T: Now who has decided what part to draw first?

C: I'm going to draw the bulb part.

T: Okay, what kind of lines will you use?

C: Curvy ones.

T: Great! Who will start with a different part?

C: I will make the bowl first.

T: Yes, that's another way to start.

SHARING AND REFLECTING:

T: I see lots of different kinds of lines people used in these drawings (Figure 3.2a, b, and c). Can you find a drawing where the artist made very light lines? How did Vanessa make lines to show the edge of the bowl (Figure 3.2a)? What kinds of lines did anyone use to show the pebbles? Who made really dark lines? Who can show me where the same kind of line was made over and over again?

Evaluation: What kinds of marks and lines did students use to represent bulbs and their parts? Were they able to use varying line weights and qualities to represent thick, thin, bumpy, and smooth parts?

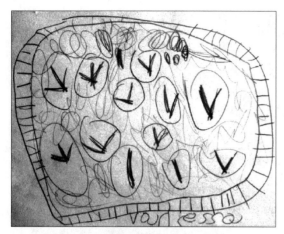

FIG. 3.2A: *Narcissi*, Vanessa, Pre-kindergarten.

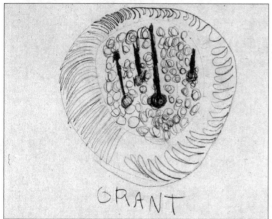

FIG. 3.2B: *Narcissi*, Grant, Kindergarten.

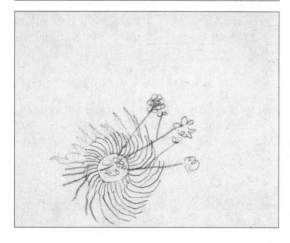

FIG. 3.2C: *Narcissi*, Daniel, Kindergarten.

Extensions: This lesson can be expanded in conjunction with a science lesson on observing how things change when they grow. Students can make drawings of the bulbs right after they are planted in the bowl. They can draw them again after the bulbs have sprouted and once more when the flowers are blooming. The drawings can be displayed so the children can observe the recorded changes.

As an alternative, bulbs could be planted at different times so all the stages of growth are seen and can be drawn at the same time. Bulbs in various stages could be cut in half so that children can see what's inside, examine and compare them, and draw the cross-section of each stage.

A bowl of blooming bulbs could be placed in the painting corner to inspire the children to do an observation painting. The paint will encourage them to look and consider the different colors as well as shapes.

OUTSIDE CLIMBING STRUCTURE

These structures are played on every day at recess. Children are very familiar with them.

Objective: Learning to Look: To learn to look at shapes and edges of all the parts of the playground equipment and to consider ways to translate what is seen into a drawing of various sorts of lines and shapes.

Materials: 9" x 12" white drawing paper, pencils, erasers, and a clipboard or some other hard portable surface on which to draw.

Room Arrangement: Children are outside on a calm, mild day sitting together in a group facing the different pieces of playground equipment.

Motivational Dialogue

TOPIC QUESTION:
>   *T:* What is your favorite place to play out here on the playground?
>   *C:* I like to climb on the ladder and swing on the rings.
>   *C:* My favorite is the slide.
>   *C:* I hide behind that part.

ASSOCIATION:
>   *T:* Let's look at the swing set and then you tell me the parts you see.
>   *C:* There's the big high bar that holds up the swings.

C: And the half circles that you sit on and those little rings where the chains attach.

T: Good, and what about the climbing structure?

C: There's the ladder part and all the bars and the rings and the slide.

VISUALIZATION:

T: There are lots of parts with different shapes and lines. Can you draw in the air with your finger to show the part that holds up the swings?

C: Like this! (The child makes in the air two large upside down "V" shapes connected by a horizontal line.)

T: Yes, that's a good way to make that! How about the part where you sit? What kind of lines or shapes could you use?

C: I'd make a curvy line for the seats.

T: Can you tell me where you would make lots of straight or slanty lines?

C: I'd make some for the slide and the ladder.

C: The grass.

T: Who can show me how to draw the edge of the slide?

C: I can. It would go like this! (Child makes a line in air with her finger.)

TRANSITION:

T: Find a good spot to sit so you can see what you want to draw. Who knows which piece of equipment they are going to draw? (Children raise their hands.)

T: Good! Who is going to start by making a shape for part of the climbing structure? Who will start by making a line to show the edge? Where is the best place on your paper to start your line or make the shape?

SHARING AND REFLECTING:

T: How did Jessica (Figure 3.3b) show grass in her drawing? Find a drawing that shows lots of long lines and lots of short lines. Who made lines go all one direction? Who used a special line to show the edge of something? If you look at Sean's drawing, how can you tell the ladder is very tall (Figure 3.3c)?

Evaluation: Did students show contour by drawing the edge of some of the parts? Did some students' work describe the many different parts of the equipment they were drawing? In the sharing session, did students notice the different ways lines were organized?

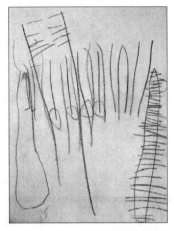

FIG. 3.3A: Climbing Structure, Justin, Kindergarten.

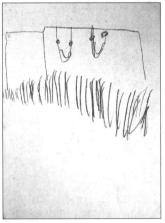

FIG. 3.3B: Swing Set, Jessica, Kindergarten.

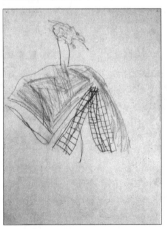

FIG. 3.3C: Hill, Tree, Ladder, Sean, Kindergarten.

Extensions: Climbing structures are wonderful subjects for three-dimensional paper construction. After children have experimented with different paper strips and shapes, making them stand up and stick out by bending and folding, they could observe and construct a piece of playground equipment.

Children enjoy going outside to draw. A lesson drawing cars parked outside the school is another inviting way to emphasize curves and contours.

THREE-HEADED DRAGON

Objective: Expression: To learn to include some of the expressive qualities of the object. The dragon has the following expressive qualities: movement in the necks and body, jagged teeth, plates down the spine, scaly texture, and a heavy, massive body. (Children respond to this toy's fierce qualities when they use it in play.)

Materials: 9" x 12" white drawing paper, pencils, and erasers.

Room Arrangement: Children are seated around a table with a plastic dragon in the middle.

Motivational Dialogue

Topic Question:
    T: Who likes to play with this toy dragon? (Most children raise their hands.)

The three association and visualization questions that follow help break down the task of reaching this lesson's more complex objective.

Association Question 1:
    T: Does the dragon have any scary parts?
    C: The teeth.

Visualization:
    T: What shape are the teeth?
    C: They are all pointy.
    T: Are there any other jagged parts on the dragon?
    C: The bumps on the back.
    T: When you draw those, what kind of line will you use?
    C: A zig-zag line.

T: What kind of pointy, scary line can you draw in the air with your finger? (Child sketches in air.)

ASSOCIATION QUESTION 2:
T: Does the dragon have any big parts?
C: The body.

VISUALIZATION:
T: What kind of shape will you draw to show how big and heavy the dragon's body is? (Child makes a circle with arms.)

ASSOCIATION QUESTION 3:
T: Does the dragon have any curvy, swoopy parts?
C: All the necks.
T: Any other part?
C: The back where the bumps are.

VISUALIZATION:
T: What kinds of lines will you draw to show the swoopy parts?
C: One like this! (Child makes arclike gesture.)

TRANSITION:
T: What part are you going to draw first? Will you draw the body or the necks first?
C: The body.
T: Good. Who is going to start with a neck or another part? (Child raises hand.)
T: Good. Think about where to put your pencil on the paper and start.

SHARING AND REFLECTING:
T: Who made the body very big and heavy looking (Figure 3.4a)? Who made the dragon look scary (Figure 3.4c)? How? Can you find some part where you used very curvy, swoopy lines (Figure 3.4b)? Who can show the biggest and the smallest parts you made?

Evaluation: Were the children able to show some of the dragon's expressive features? Which ones? Do the drawings show size differences to contrast the big and little parts? Did any children make lines or marks to show the texture of the plates down the dragon's spine?

Extensions: The expressive qualities of certain objects can also be captured in color. An observation painting could be done of the dragon. Other expressive objects to paint might be models of dinosaurs or unusual flowers, such as a bird of paradise.

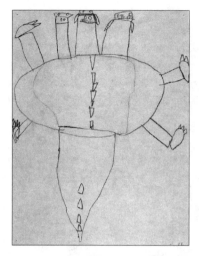

FIG. 3.4A: *3-Headed Dragon*, William, Kindergarten.

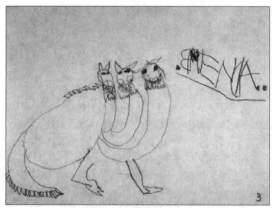

FIG. 3.4B: *3-Headed Dragon*, Brenda, Kindergarten.

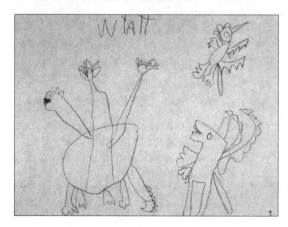

FIG. 3.4C: *3-Headed Dragon*, Wyatt, Kindergarten.

four

First and Second Grades

DEVELOPMENTAL FRAMEWORK

Six- and 7-year-olds are embarking on a journey of exploration, expanding their boundaries and organizing their worlds of objects and experiences. They are beginning to apply logical reasoning and to make distinctions between groups and categories, creating hierarchies within them. They engage in diverse activities with inexhaustible energy and curiosity and are anxious to talk about their discoveries and insights.

Children at this age are becoming more selective about their friends, forming social groups and exclusive relationships. Fighting and making up are part of a normal day. While at times they are gregarious, these same children can remain focused on quiet tasks. They are acquiring reading and writing skills that make them feel grown-up. Yet they retain their need for security.

Representation

Children's drawing continues to reflect their increasing cognitive abilities. Since it is now easier for them to differentiate and reflect on elements of their experience, they more readily separate components of the drawing task, such as observing an object and manipulating drawing materials. Here we see a significant developmental shift from the previous stage of the 4- and 5-year-old.

Between the ages of 6 and 7, as children begin to think logically, we see them form concepts of classes and categories. These new cognitive abilities are reflected in their representations. Compared with the earlier, more generalized pictures of 4- and 5-year-olds, drawings at this stage are more differentiated and specific. Characteristics that designate how objects are similar and different are becoming increasingly important, and drawings are likely to include more attributes specific to the object being represented. A closer match develops between what is perceived about an object and what is shown in drawing. Observation drawings reveal that children are paying attention to shape, relative size, placement, and number of parts. The children may include some subtle details in their drawings. Also, they may draw shapes within shapes and attach shapes to one another. Some children may follow the contour of the observed object.

In Amanda's drawing of a cactus (Figure 4.3a), she draws shapes to show the main stem and its smaller segments. She uses her pencil with care to show length, direction, placement, and texture of the cactus needles. Compare the generalized use of curved and straight lines and the omission of the central enclosed carapace shape in Frankie's lobster drawing (Figure 4.2a) with the more articulated use of shape, line, and inclusion of parts in Gabriel's (Figure 4.2b). Amanda draws her cactus with steady, composed lines and shapes (Figure 4.3a), but Scott's are rough and loose (Figure 4.3b). Jessie skillfully observes contours and assembles shapes when she draws the trike (Figure 4.5a). Ariel's drawing of a car is a tight unit of shapes that show its contour (Figure 4.6a). Within that unit she places windows, doors, and door handles and attaches the ski rack on top.

Many children at this age like to include a story in their observation drawings by adding parts from memory. For example, Laura parks her car in front of a building (Figure 4.6b), and Jenny places hers traveling down a tree-lined highway (Figure 4.6c).

Aesthetics

As with 4- and 5-year-olds, 6- and 7-year-olds respond naturally to action, movement, and expressive features in objects. But changes are beginning to occur. Children show these in how they use marks, lines, and shapes on paper. Marks range from dark to light, slow to fast, and at times repetitive mark-making takes on the appearance of surface texture. Lines are active and energetic. They are beginning to show more variations in movement, direction, rhythm, and weight. Shapes convey movement and weight with a growing tendency toward stability.

In her lobster drawing (Figure 4.2c), Merle captures the large and curving quality of the claw by carefully drawing a smooth, massive shape in the center of her paper. She modulates the pressure of her pencil as she adds a jagged, toothlike line to show its sharp inside edge. Sarah draws a squat, flat, square shape and shades deliberately along its outside edge, suggesting the heavy quality of the cactus pot (Figure 4.3c). She attaches a lumpy shape for the cactus that changes from dark to light as she navigates its outer edge with her pencil. She bears down hard to show little holes on the cactus's surface and adds quick, sharp repetitive lines in many directions to indicate its spiny needles.

Four- and 5-year-olds generally record their response in the moment, whereas 6- and 7-year-olds reflect on the process of responding and drawing. They capture aesthetic qualities in their drawings, although they are not aware they are doing so. Teachers can help students make vital connections between expressive qualities in the object and the expressive possibilities of the material through dialogue during the drawing process and through sharing and reflecting afterward. They can assist them in making aesthetic qualities become an important part of the drawing experience.

Concepts of the Material

Children enjoy using a variety of art materials and respond naturally to their diverse qualities. To use any material fluently, a child must have adequate time to manipulate and explore it. A delicate balance exists between object and materials, and a child must see a relationship between them in order to articulate meaning.

At this age, children are beginning to develop a drawing repertoire of marks, lines, and shapes based on earlier explorations. They can move their pencil on paper with intention and predict a result. They are beginning to control and coordinate the direction and length of lines, delineate the contours of a variety of shapes, control pressure to create areas of dark and light, and combine marks, lines, and shapes by connecting them on the page. They are starting to erase and change parts of their drawings that do not satisfy them.

In Rebecca's tricycle drawing (Figure 4.5b), she carefully controls the direction of her lines to show the handlebars, bike frame, seat, and tire spokes. Erasures reveal changes made in the lines used to represent the length of the handlebars and placement of the seat. Jessie describes the dark wheels by bearing down hard while following their round shape (Figure 4.5a). Scott creates a range of light and dark tones by changing the pressure of the pencil on the page in his drawing of a cactus (Figure 4.3b).

Teachers can help children control the different ways they are using materials by noticing and talking to them about what they have done and how that shows in their pictures. It is important for teachers to help children develop concepts of materials so they will be able to translate their growing perceptions of objects into their drawings.

Objects to Draw

Four factors are important to consider when choosing objects for 6- and 7-year-old children to draw. First, the object should be compelling. Children at this age are interested in things encountered in their daily lives. Appropriate subjects for drawing are my best friend, my favorite toy, my house, my pet, or other familiar objects. Unique objects such as a Venus's-flytrap, a stuffed (real) animal, or an exotic toy from another country are also of interest. Once a teacher gets to know his students' interests, he can select objects accordingly.

Second, the teacher should select objects that match the drawing skills of 6- and 7-year-old children. Objects that are too complex can be frustrating and will discourage children's enthusiasm about observation drawing. It is wise to start out with objects that are easy to break down into simple parts, that have easy-to-follow contours, or that have obvious expressive or salient qualities.

Third, when choosing an object for 6- and 7-year-olds to draw, the teacher should make sure that the object corresponds clearly to the learning objective. A carefully thought-out match with a clear and focused motivational dialogue can help children at this age concentrate on the drawing task. For example, if the learning objective is to have children translate parts observed in an object into shapes in a drawing, then the object chosen should be composed of distinct shapes, like a car or house. If the learning objective is to translate texture into marks and lines, then the object should have obvious textural qualities, like the furriness of a rabbit or the prickly spines of a cactus. Matches such as these along with succinct motivational questions enable children to connect with the drawing task.

Finally, at this age level the object and material chosen for drawing should have a clear and concrete correspondence. A lead pencil is appropriate for drawing an object that is linear or has hard, distinct parts; oil pastels are appropriate if the edges of an object are blended and subtle.

Problems and Responses

Teachers need to recognize and address the important task of helping children develop new strategies to apply to observation drawing. Strategies that were suitable earlier may no longer suffice. And the teacher may need to give additional attention to children who are having difficulty getting started.

Pointed questions can encourage children to choose specific drawing strategies. For example, asking, "What kind of shape would you like to draw to show the wheel?" may help a child begin to identify basic shapes and parts of a bicycle. Asking, "What kind of line would you like to draw to show the round part of the bird's back?" might help a child start to delineate contours. Questions such as, "Where do you want to place the shape on your paper?" or, "How do you think you can get the bicycle wheel to join the frame?" can lead a child to notice how parts fit together to make up the whole. Asking, "How can you show that the scales of the stegosaurus are sharp and bristling?" may get a child to respond to expressive or salient qualities of the object.

Having a child trace part of an object's contour in the air while paying attention to how it feels as he follows the changing edge helps him connect to the drawing process. The teacher can guide the child to move his finger from the air to the paper. Usually he then can draw the observed edge with his pencil.

Sometimes children have trouble manipulating the drawing material to correspond with what they perceive about an object. For example, Edith tries to control the length, direction, and quality of the line she uses to show the saw's blade and has to erase before she gets it the way she wants (Figure 4.1). Reminding children to slow down as they draw helps them think about where they want to make the pencil go on the paper. Pointing out that they can stop drawing and start up again helps them gain more control.

Children at this age tend to think that they need to erase everything and start all over when something does not look right to them. A teacher can guide a child to identify the part of the drawing she wants to erase. Asking sensitive questions like, "What doesn't look right?" or, "Which part do you want to draw over?" may help a child be specific about changes she wants to make. Children also may have trouble regulating the pressure they exert on their pencils and make lines that are too hard to erase. Gentle reminders to draw lightly at first will help them become more aware.

Teachers need to respect the challenges posed by observation drawing. Responsive feedback helps children become more confident. For example, it is not uncommon to hear a frustrated child exclaim, "I don't like this!" A teacher can respond by describing something the child has done, such as, "You have made a large, curving shape and attached a sharp zig-zag line to show the lobster's claw. What do you want to draw next?" Similar comments encourage children to identify what they have drawn and focus them on how to continue. Interactions between teacher and child build trust and deepen the drawing experience.

LESSON PLANS

WOODWORKING TOOLS: FIRST GRADE

Objective: Learning to Look: To learn that familiar objects can be broken down into basic parts and how these parts can be translated into lines and shapes on paper.

Materials: 12" x 18" white drawing paper, pencils, and erasers.

Room Arrangement: Children are seated in a large circle with their work tables set up behind them. A saw, hammer, goggles, and portable vise are arranged on a low surface in the middle of the circle.

Motivational Dialogue

TOPIC QUESTION:
   T: I bet everyone can name these tools. Who would like to try?
   C: A saw, hammer, goggles, and the holding thing.
   T: Yes, it's a vise, Tim. Good.

ASSOCIATION QUESTION 1:
   T: Now who can tell me how we use these tools?
   C: The saw cuts the wood, the hammer helps nail, and the goggles we wear.
   T: What about the vise?
   C: It holds the wood.

VISUALIZATION:
   T: We are going to draw these tools. What are some of their special parts?
   C: The sharp pointed part of the saw.
   T: Right. And Max, what shape would you make that part?
   C: Kind of a long triangle.
   T: Good. How would you make a line to show the saws sharp teeth?
   C: I would do it like this. (Child shows the motion of a zig-zag line in the air.)

ASSOCIATION QUESTION 2:
   T: Fine. Who can describe another special tool part?
   C: The eye part of the goggles.

VISUALIZATION:

    T: Yes, and what shape are they?

    C: Round, two round circles, next to each other, with little circles on the sides (vent holes in plastic).

    T: Right. Good looking, Sue. How would you draw the straps on the goggles? What kinds of lines would you use?

    C: I'd use wavy lines.

    T: Okay, and where would you start your wavy line, Sean?

    C: On one side and then go to the other side.

TRANSITION:

    T: Now, I want you to raise your hand and tell me which tool you are going to draw first.

    C: The saw.

    T: And which part will you make first?

    C: The handle.

    T: What shape will you make it?

    C: Kind of square with a wiggly hole in it.

    T: Great. Who is going to start with a different tool?

    C: Do we have to draw them all?

    T: (Sensing she's overwhelmed) Some of you may take all the time to draw one tool very carefully, and some will have time to draw all of them. There is no rule that says you have to draw them all. Which one will you choose to draw, Ann?

    C: The hammer.

    T: Okay, and which part will you make first?

    C: The handle.

    T: Good. Show me in the air how you might make the shape of the handle. (Ann moves her finger in the air.) Okay! Everyone think as you move to your table to draw, which part of the tool will you make first, and how will you make it on your paper.

SHARING AND REFLECTING:

    T: What shape did Meredith use to show the handle of the saw? What kind of line did Edith use to show the edge of the saw's blade (Figure 4.1)? What shapes did Sue use to show the goggles? What kinds of lines did Sean use to draw the straps?

Evaluation: Were the children able to identify the basic parts of the tools? Could they translate these parts into lines and shapes on paper?

Extensions: Children can draw other workbench tools, kitchen utensils, clockworks, and mechanical gadgets.

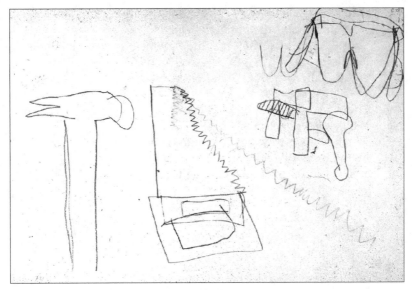

FIG. 4.1: Woodworking Tool, Edith, Grade One.

LOBSTER: FIRST GRADE

Objective: Learning to Look: To learn that parts of a lobster can be translated into marks, lines, and shapes.

Materials: 12" x 18" white drawing paper, pencils, and erasers.

Room Arrangement: Children have pushed their desks so they are close enough to view the lobster that has been placed in the center of the room.

Motivational Dialogue

TOPIC QUESTION:
    T: How many of you have seen a lobster as big as this one?
    C: That's the biggest one that I've ever seen! (Other children agree.)

ASSOCIATION:
    T: Let's look at its parts. Who can tell what some are?
    C: The claws, head, body, and tail.
    T: Are the claws the same or different?

C: One is bigger.
C: They aren't exactly the same shape either.
T: That's a good observation. Does anyone see any small parts or details?
C: Under it there are lots of little legs.
T: Yes! Anything else?
C: There are little teeth on the edge of the claw.
C: It has antennas, too.
T: Where does the lobster have parts that bend?
C: Its tail is bending. So are the legs.
T: Yes, I see that they are bending, too.

VISUALIZATION:
T: What kind of shape will you draw for the biggest claw?
C: I'm going to make it big and sort of oval with a big kind of a "V" in the front.
T: Can anyone think of a way to show the little teeth on the claw's edge?
C: I am going to make a zig-zaggy, pointy line. (Child draws in the air while describing.)
T: What shape will you draw to show the tail?
C: It's kind of like a fan with little lines in it.
T: Great. Does anyone see other places where there are lines?
C: I see lines on the body and on the legs, too.
T: Are there any parts of the lobster that you will want to make dark with your pencil?
C: Where the lines are.
C: I'm going to make the whole lobster dark.

TRANSITION:
T: Sounds like you have good ideas. Are you ready to start drawing? Think about which part you want to draw first. Where will you put your first shape on the paper?

SHARING AND REFLECTING:
T: What kind of shape did Merle draw to show the lobster's big claw (Figure 4.2c)? How did she show the teeth on its edge? How did Frankie show the claws and teeth (Figure 4.2a)? What did Gabriel do to show that the tail of the lobster was bending (Figure 4.2b)? How about the legs? How did Crystal show the bends in the lobster's legs (Figure 4.2d)? Which drawing looks dark?

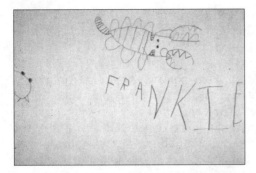

FIG. 4.2A: *Lobster,* Frankie, Grade One.

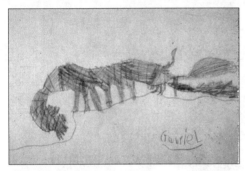

FIG. 4.2B: *Lobster,* Gabriel, Grade One.

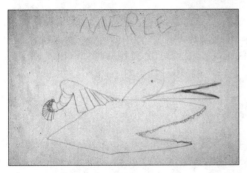

FIG. 4.2C: *Lobster,* Merle, Grade One.

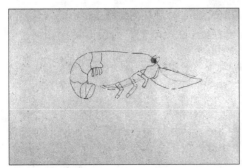

FIG. 4.2D: *Lobster,* Crystal, Grade One.

Evaluation: Did the children show the distinct parts of the lobster through the use of marks, lines, and shapes? How were their approaches to the task similar? How were they different?

Extensions: Now that the children have explored the lobster in a two-dimensional drawing, another lesson might be to have them do a three-dimensional translation into clay. The completed clay lobsters could be fired and painted. This experience could be developed into a unit on marine life by having the children make a habitat for their lobsters out of three-dimensional collage materials.

CACTUS PLANTS: FIRST GRADE

Objective: Expression: To learn that similarities and differences in the sizes, shapes, and expressive qualities of a variety of cactus plants can be translated into pencil drawings of a specific cactus.

Materials: 12" x 18" white drawing paper, pencils, and erasers.

Room Arrangement: Children have pushed their desks into groups of threes and fours. Several cactus plants have been arranged in a central place in the classroom. Before it is time to draw, one child from each group will come up and select a cactus plant for that group.

Motivational Dialogue

TOPIC QUESTION:
    T: Does anybody know what kinds of plants these are? Where do they grow? How are they different from other plants?

ASSOCIATION:
    T: (Holding up two different cactus plants) Who sees a way that these two cactus plants are different?
    C: That one is fat and round, the other one is tall and skinny.
    T: Yes, they have different shapes. How else are they different?
    C: The spikes on that one are long and sharp, and on the other one they are short and don't look as sharp. They look kind of fuzzy.
    T: They do look fuzzy on this one. Does anyone notice how else the cactus needles are different?

C: Those go straight up and down in rows, and the other has them in little bunches.

T: What do you notice about the pots the cactus plants are in?

C: That one is skinny at the bottom and fat at the top. The other one is straight up and down.

This comparative questioning can be repeated using different cactus plants to help children notice a wider range of characteristics.

VISUALIZATION:

T: If you want to show that this cactus is round and fat, what kind of shape will you draw on your paper?

C: I will draw a big, fat, oval shape.

T: Can you think of a way to show that some of the needles on this cactus are long and some are short?

C: I'll use lots of lines and make some of them longer and some of them shorter.

T: How will you use your pencil to show the sharp spiky needles and the short fuzzy ones?

C: I am going to press hard for the sharp ones and soft for the ones that are fuzzy.

T: How can you show that this cactus pot is fat at the top and skinnier at the bottom?

C: I can make the sides go up and out to the top. (Child makes gestures with a finger in the air to indicate line direction.)

Children are called to select a cactus plant and position it in the middle of their group.

TRANSITION:

T: Which part will you draw first? Where will you place it on the paper?

SHARING AND REFLECTING:

T: How did Sarah show that the cactus was short and fat (Figure 4.3c)? What kind of lines did Amanda use to make the cactus needles (Figure 4.3a)? And how did she show that some of the cactus needles were long and some were short? How did Scott show that the cactus pot was fatter at the top than at the bottom (Figure 4.3b)?

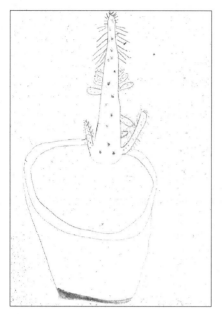

FIG. 4.3A: *Cactus*, Amanda, Grade One.

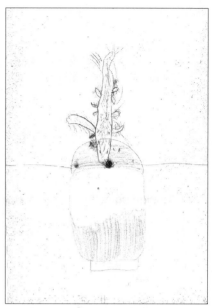

FIG. 4.3B: *Cactus*, Scott, Grade One.

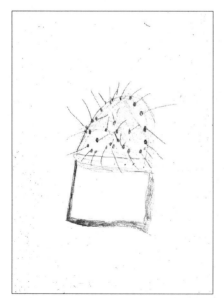

FIG. 4.3C: *Cactus*, Sarah, Grade One.

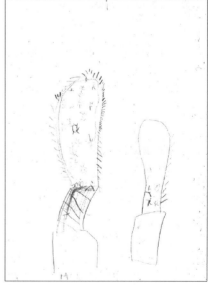

FIG. 4.3D: *Cactus*, Michael, Grade One.

Evaluation: Did the children notice and record expressive attributes of the cactus plants they were drawing? Which attributes did they pay most attention to? Did they have difficulty translating information into the drawing? If so, what kinds of trouble did they have?

Extensions: Extensions could include cut-paper collage or paintings of cactus plants. These additional experiences expand children's concepts of the expressive qualities of materials. Other extensions could be making drawings of different objects that have obvious expressive qualities, such as insects or dinosaurs.

DAFFODILS: FIRST GRADE

Objective: Space: To learn that the appearance of a simple object changes as it is seen from different views, which can be translated from observations into drawings.

Materials: 9" x 12" white drawing paper, pencils, and erasers.

Room Arrangement: Children are seated on the floor in a group with the teacher. Their desks are set up for drawing, and a daffodil has been placed on each desk.

Motivational Dialogue

TOPIC QUESTION:
    T: I have brought each one of you a spring flower to draw. Let's look at mine. Do you know what kind of flower this is or what it is called?
    C: It's a daffodil, a jonquil. We have them in our garden.

ASSOCIATION:
    T: That's right. Let's look at it very carefully to see all its parts and think about ways we could draw it. What part can you name?
    C: I see the stem, the petals, and the fuzzy, thin, brown part.
    T: Good. Now who can tell me some of the other parts?
    C: The two kinds of petals, the flat ones and the middle stick-out one.
    T: Good. Now we have named all the parts we can see.
    C: No, there are little, special parts inside the middle petal.
    T: Nice observation. Can everybody see inside the middle petal?

C: No, I can't see it. You have to turn it to let me see the inside.

T: That's true. You can't see the inside of the daffodil from where you are sitting. I have to turn it. Does it look different when I turn it around?

C: Yes. Now we can see the brown, wrinkly part in the back.

T: Can you see that part if I turn it like this? (Teacher turns the opening of the daffodil toward the child.)

C: Yes, a little, but the petals hide it.

T: Now I have a hard question to ask. When I turn the daffodil this way, who sees any round shapes? (Some of the children who can see the front of the daffodil raise their hands.)

T: Okay. Do you see a round shape, Sonia?

C: (Sonia is looking at the daffodil from the side.) No, it looks kind of square with ruffles.

T: Terrific. You are really looking carefully. If I turn the daffodil around again, will other people see different sides or views?

C: Yes.

T: Well, then if I turn the daffodil different ways, different parts show, and they may be a different shape, too. What do the smaller petals look like from the front of the daffodil?

C: They look like triangles and go out from the big one.

T: Does the stem look the same from there?

C: Yes, pretty much the same.

T: Hmm. Then we really have to look carefully to see what this flower looks like from each side.

VISUALIZATION:

T: Now, when you draw your daffodil, you will have to decide first what way you will hold it and find out which parts you can see. Then you will have to think about what kinds of shapes you will draw to show those parts. What will you do first?

C: Well, I will draw it from the front and make a long shape for the stem first.

T: That's a good idea. Will anybody draw something else at first?

C: I'll draw the big round petal first.

T: Will you be looking at the front or the side of the big petal?

C: The front. But I'll make the back part, too

TRANSITION:

T: Okay. Let's go back to our seats and draw the daffodil from different views. Which side will you look at first, and what parts and shapes will you make first?

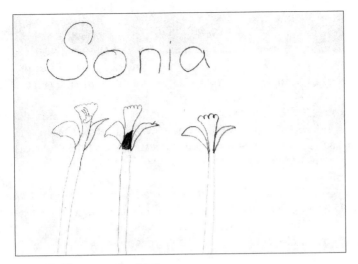

FIG. 4.4A: *Daffodil*, Sonia, Grade One.

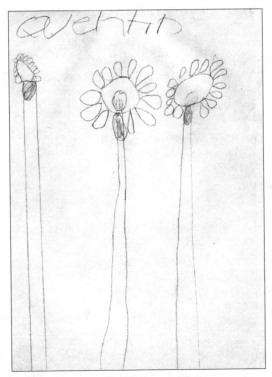

FIG. 4.4B: *Daffodil*, Quentin, Grade One.

SHARING AND REFLECTING:

> T: Which sides of the daffodil did Sonia draw (Figure 4.4a)? Do they look the same or different? How are they different? How does the stem change in another drawing? How about the petals? Which parts changed in Quentin's drawing (Figure 4.4b)?

Evaluation: Did the children draw the daffodil from different views? Did the parts and shapes change from one view to another? Which views did they choose to draw? Was one view easier for the children to draw than another? Were they interested in the task?

Extensions: A follow-up lesson could be to have the children do the daffodil again from different views using cut-paper collage. This would give them an opportunity to use what they learned from drawing and get them to hone in more closely on parts and shapes.

TRICYCLE: SECOND GRADE

Objective: Learning to Look: To learn that the parts of a tricycle connect and can be translated into connecting shapes on paper.

Materials: 12" x 18" white drawing paper, pencils, and erasers.

Room Arrangement: Children are seated in a circle around a tricycle. Their work tables are behind them.

Motivational Dialogue

TOPIC QUESTION:

> T: Who remembers riding this kind of bike when they were little? (Lots of hands go up.)
> T: What is this kind of bike called?
> C: It's a trike. Three-wheeler. Tricycle.
> T: Yes, because it has three wheels.

ASSOCIATION:

> T: How are the wheels the same or different?
> C: There are two small wheels in the back and a big one up front.
> T: Why does the trike have two small wheels in the back?
> C: They help you balance.

T: What does the big wheel up front do?

C: It helps you steer the bike.

T: That's true. What other parts help you steer?

C: The handlebars.

T: Can you tell how they are connected to the rest of the trike?

C: The skinny parts on either side of the wheel touch the same part the handlebar touches.

T: What other part of the trike is connected to the front wheel?

C: The pedals are.

T: Which part of the bike is in between the front and back wheels?

C: The seat.

VISUALIZATION:

T: What kind of shapes will you draw for the wheels of the trike?

C: I will draw a big circle shape for the front and two small ones for the back.

T: Which shapes will you connect to the front-wheel shape?

C: The pedals.

T: Yes, and how will you draw their shape?

C: Like a shoe.

T: Do you see any special part that connects them to the wheel?

C: Yes, it's that skinny metal part. I will have to draw that shape and connect it to the wheel.

T: What kind of shape will you draw to show the seat?

C: A fat and curved one.

T: What parts will it connect to?

C: The round part near the handlebars.

T: Does it connect anywhere else?

C: Yes, to the footrest in the back.

TRANSITION:

T: Which part of the trike will you draw first? Where will you place it on the paper? Which part of the trike will you draw next, and how will you connect it to the first part?

SHARING AND REFLECTING:

T: What shapes did Rebecca draw to show the wheels of the trike (Figure 4.5b)? Which wheel is the biggest? How did Jessie show that the front wheel connects to the handlebars (Figure 4.5a)? How would you describe the shape she used for the handlebars? What shape connects the handlebars to the rest of the bike? Whose drawing has a line that's smooth in one place and bumpy in another?

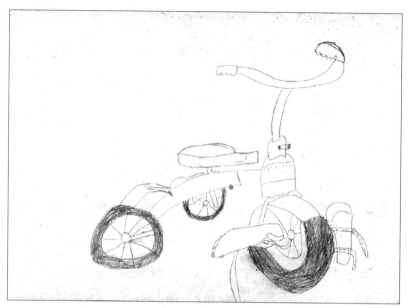

FIG. 4.5A: Tricycle, Jessie, Grade Two.

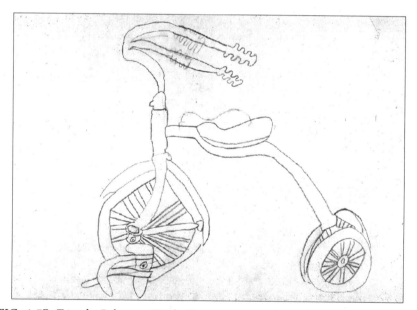

FIG. 4.5B: Tricycle, Rebecca, Grade Two.

Evaluation: Have the children paid attention to the parts of the trike and translated them into shapes in their drawings? Have they shown how these shapes are connected? While sharing, were the children able to identify where connections between parts were made? Did they notice where different kinds of lines were used?

Extensions: Children could continue to explore how parts connect by drawing simple mechanical objects. This could be followed by creating three-dimensional constructions in which one or more of the connected parts can move. Children could then do observation drawings of their own constructions.

CARS: SECOND GRADE

Objective: Learning to Look: To learn that a car can be translated into organized and related shapes, with smaller shapes nested within larger ones that make up the whole.

Materials: Drawing boards, 9" x 12" or larger white drawing paper, pencils, and erasers.

Room Arrangement: Children are working in a safe place in the school parking lot where they can see several different cars.

Motivational Dialogue: (Children are gathered in a central place to view one car.)

TOPIC QUESTION:
    T: Has anyone ever seen a car like this one?
    C: My uncle has one like it. He drove us to camp in it.
    C: My nex-door neighbor has a car that looks like that, but it's red.

ASSOCIATION:
    T: Who can come up and trace with a finger all around the car to show its shape? (Hands go up. The teacher picks one child, who goes up to the care and points all around its shape.) That is a very large shape, isn't it? Let's look closely at some of the parts of the car. What is another large part that you can see?
    C: The door.

T: Go up and point all around the shape of the door so that we all
    can see. (Child goes up and outlines the edge of the door with
    her finger.)

T: Does anyone see another part inside the door part?

C: I see the window and the door handle.

T: Go up and point around the window shape for us.

C: (Child goes up and traces around the edge of the window.) And
    the back window is here (indicating the edge).

T: Good. Now let's look very closely at the door handle. Does any-
    one see any small parts inside?

C: There is the place where you put the key in. It's a circle with a
    little hole inside.

T: Yes, and how can you describe the shape of that part?

C: It's bumpy.

T: Let's take a look at the wheels. We can see that they are round.
    Does anyone see any smaller parts inside the big wheel shape?

C: I see the hubcap. It's round, too.

VISUALIZATION:

T: How will you draw the outside shape of this car?

C: It will be a square shape with that bumper part poking out.

C: The top is round, and then it gets square again like in the front.

T: What kind of shape will you make to show the door?

C: It's kind of square at the bottom, and it gets rounder at the top.

T: What shapes will you put inside the door shape?

C: I will add the window.

T: How will you draw it?

C: It's flat at the bottom and then round.

T: Is there anything else you will add inside the shape of the door?

C: The little rectangle shapes for the door handles.

T: Who has an idea about how they will show the wheel and hub-
    cap?

C: I will draw a round shape for the wheel and then put a smaller
    one inside.

TRANSITION:

T: Now it's time to choose the car you want to draw. Some of you
    might want to stay here and draw the car we have been talking
    about, and some of you might want to draw another one. When
    you are ready to draw, think about whether you will start with an
    outside shape or an inside shape. Decide what part you will
    draw first and how to show it on your paper. (Note: The children

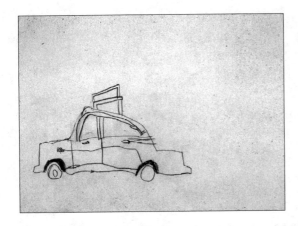

FIG. 4.6A: *Car*, Ariel, Grade Two.

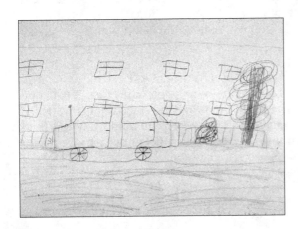

FIG. 4.6B: *Car*, Laura.

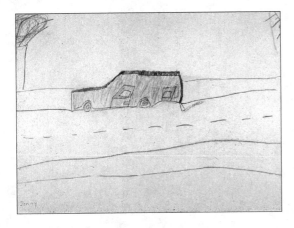

FIG. 4.6C: *Car*, Jenny.

should get situated quickly so that they do not get distracted. Since they will be spreading out, it is important that the teacher walk around, checking to make sure each child is safe and focused on task.)

SHARING AND REFLECTING:

T: Laura made a large shape to show the car in her picture (Figure 4.6b). What other parts did she draw? What shapes did she use? Are there little parts inside of big parts? What shape did Ariel use to show the front door (Figure 4.6a)? What shapes did she put inside? Do you see a drawing where someone showed the hub-cap of the wheel? How did that person show the hubcap?

Evaluation: Were the children able to differentiate the parts of the car and translate these parts into shapes? Were they able to see small parts inside of large parts and translate these into little shapes inside of bigger shapes?

Extensions: The children could use their drawings as a reference to make a cut-paper collage. This would give them the opportunity to translate and manipulate the parts and shapes in their drawings by cutting, arranging, and overlapping. Other related subjects for observation drawing could include toy cars, trucks, trains, and rockets; model airplanes; and toy or model boats.

five

Third and Fourth Grades

DEVELOPMENTAL FRAMEWORK

Eight- and 9-year-olds are at ease with ideas and social relationships as well as action. Their large muscle coordination is sufficient to ride a bike, learn gymnastic stunts, and participate in team sports with energy and skill. In idle moments, they hone small muscle skills by picking up objects with their toes or twisting their faces into intricate grimaces. They learn about the world of objects by collecting and sorting toy cars, pebbles, stickers, and scraps of fabric. In a similar fashion, they explore natural phenomena by testing them physically: poking at ice forming at the edge of a puddle, running into the wind, or dancing before it. Their knowledge of the world is encyclopedic, nourished by their incessant curiosity.

Their social horizons are expanding as well. Children who worked alone a year or two ago will now maneuver fiercely to be with favored friends. Acceptance or rejection can color the experience of a day or a lifetime. Although they form tight social groups with their age-mates, older role models also shape their aspirations and behavior. They tag after the upper-grade children, mimicking their actions, begging to be included. They avidly follow adult heroes and villains, particularly sports and entertainment celebrities. These figures inhabit fantasy play and growing notions of the adult world.

Representation

Substantial changes are apparent in the 8- and 9-year-old's drawing strategies. These changes occur both in the child's treatment of individual parts and in the relationship of parts to the whole. Five- and 6-year-olds usually construct a drawing by juxtaposing basic shapes. With development, children enclose several shapes with a single contour line, while leaving others distinct. They also modify basic shapes, making them increasingly specific. Eventually, they begin to use an enclosing contour that travels around the entire object. They indicate individual parts by modulating the contour.

The use of an enclosing contour line creates an overall effect of wholeness in the drawing and marks the most significant transition in 8- and 9-year-olds' approach to drawing. Compare the lobster (Figure 4.2a) produced by Frankie, age 6, with the pheasant (Figure 5.3a) drawn by Barry, age 9. Frankie uses the same basic shape for the body, claws, legs, and tail of the lobster. He then subdivides or adds smaller segments, elaborating on the basic shape. He places these shapes next to each other to assemble the whole. In contrast, Barry renders the body, head, and neck of the pheasant with a single unbroken line, which changes direction to indicate individual parts: down and around the hump of the back, leveling off at the base of the tail, gently arcing to capture the curve of the long tail feathers, smoothly pushing forward to round the breast.

Other changes are now apparent. Since 8- and 9-year-olds are focusing on the object as a whole rather than cobbling parts together, they make overall proportions become more naturalistic. The children use contour to describe subtle changes in edge as well as to denote boundary. John's "worried" self-portrait (Figure 5.1a) suggests the soft swelling of cheeks and the jutting boniness of chin. In Bonnie's shell drawing (Figure 5.4a), contour lines indicate curving and flat edges, sharp angles, and rough or bumpy surfaces. At this age, children are fascinated by detail and incorporate it in their drawings enthusiastically. In Erin's pheasant drawing (Figure 5.3b), she uses strongly differentiated patterns and tones and suggests changes in texture as well. Emmanuel indicates numerous variations of edge and surface in his drawing of an abalone shell (Figure 5.4b).

Some strategies appear in the drawings of a few children at this age but will not be used commonly until fifth and sixth grade. The 6- or 7-year-old typically represents objects in a frontal or side view. The 8- and 9-year-old begins to experiment with internal contour line, overlapping, and oblique views. Jennifer uses parallel contour lines to show that her nose protrudes (Figure 5.1b). Jaclyn overlaps near and far to depict both inside and outside in her lively sandal drawing (Figure 5.5a). Wendy angles the head of her pheasant away from the viewer and into the picture plane (Figure

5.3c). All of these strategies create an illusion of mass and depth that is notably absent in the drawings of younger children. The images now appear to contain and occupy space, rather than lie flat on the paper. They reflect new understandings of the object and demonstrate the search for a powerful means to represent those understandings.

Aesthetics

Eight- and 9-year-olds' drawings show an increasing attention to the nuances of contour, pattern, surface, and tone. This interest is analytical but also deeply rooted in affective experience. The child's ability to link emotional response with more dispassionate knowledge and mark-making skills is now conscious. This awareness nourishes the ability to select and vary drawing strategies toward an aesthetic end. We see its effect in Chris's drawing of fear (Figure 5.1c). Short, feathery strokes evoke the prickly sensation of hair standing on end. Eyes bulge. Pupils constrict. Quivery lines underscore the tension in eyes and mouth. Light circular movements capture the rush of blood to the cheeks. Objects and subjects that are less charged also draw on aesthetic experience. In his sneaker drawing (Figure 5.5b), Todd contrasts the blunt, hard rubbery sole with the softer canvas enclosure of the shoe. Firm, angular lines become energetic and curving as the shoelaces emerge from their laced confinement.

Although they are not yet doing so purposefully, children are beginning to compose their drawings, placing objects carefully in relation to the paper surface and within the picture plane and selecting elements of foreground and background to create a subtle interplay of parts and whole. Humor or fantasy often provide a compositional framework, as in Elaine's egg-spilling shopper (Figure 5.2a), and Danny's enormous ice skate (Figure 5.2b). Meghan suggests a more ambiguous mood through use of tone and scale, placing her large, emphatically drawn toy panda in a repetitive, sketchy grove of trees (Figure 5.2c).

Teachers can provide support for children's investigation of the more subtle aesthetic qualities in objects. They also can help them to articulate their search for satisfying drawing strategies. This can happen during motivational discussions, when the children are encouraged to identify aspects of the object they find personally compelling. At the same time, the children can be asked to speculate on mark-making strategies they might use to capture those qualities. During the drawing session, the teacher may point out aesthetic use of materials or compositional choices: "You've made the tail feathers look very stiff with that straight line, but soft at the end where the line curves." "Drawing the bear almost as big as the trees makes it look powerful, but since it's a stuffed toy bear, it seems mysterious as well."

After the drawing session, children might be asked to assess the strategies chosen and to suggest other possible options. At this age, children particularly enjoy sharing information with others and readily adapt useful ideas from their peers. The teacher may provide an initial framework for observation and assessment by raising relevant questions, while encouraging the children to sharpen essential skills of reflection and communication. Preparatory discussions, drawing time, and summative evaluations can thus become a time for rich and productive interchange.

Concepts of the Material

Eight- and 9-year-old children continue to develop more subtle ways of using materials. Improved fine motor skills and increased awareness of detail contribute steadily to a more varied range of marks, lines, and shapes. They also are more aware of and interested in modulating the effects, such as the hardness and softness of a pencil line, that can be achieved with drawing tools. They can match these intentionally with the expressive qualities observed in their drawing objects. For example, as shown in Figure 5.3c, Wendy understands that her pencil can be used to make crisp, hard lines and soft, sketchy ones to differentiate between the stiff tail feathers and the softer, more flexible head feathers in her pheasant drawing. She is further able to link movement and pressure in her handling of the pencil to indicate texture, color, and pattern simultaneously in the jagged up-and-down markings of the bird's neck feathers.

Children of any age enjoy exploring the possibilities and limits of a material. They also need time to become familiar with the particular characteristics of each material as it is introduced. Graphite pencils, colored pencils, chalk, and cut-paper collage each offer possibilities and encourage the development of different representational strategies. Students can develop skills with a material through repeated exposure, bringing established learning to bear on a new focus of exploration.

Objects to Draw

Objects selected for drawing should further children's perceptual awareness and mark-making range. Living objects, such as plants or animals, engage them immediately. Such objects provide increasingly challenging drawing tasks, such as the development of subtlety in the handling of edge or contour, pattern and texture. Stuffed toys or matchbox cars may provide a strong affective interest, as well as encouraging attention to surface or detail. Things that offer a taste of the adult world, such as tools, kitchen gadgets, or simple machines, are equally intriguing and useful in focusing attention on proportion or depth. Going outdoors to draw in the neighborhood provides the opportunity for 8- and 9-year-olds to try on the role of adult artists. This also encourages their dawning interest in the representation of space and volume.

Lessons that engage children's growing sense of self and social interests are compelling. Children may be encouraged to explore feelings by drawing portraits to delineate the changing shapes and shifting emotional content of facial features. Figure drawing can explore human action and interaction through both gesture and placement of figures in relation to one another. Sequential lessons that move from observing single objects to objects in relation to other objects or contexts provide opportunities to enlarge children's awareness of compositional possibilities. Drawings can incorporate multiple objects as the child's conceptual and social frame of reference expands. Such extensions may be based on further observation, on memory, on fantasy, or on a combination of all three.

Matching the material to the drawing object can also further children's perceptual awareness and mark-making range. Ebony pencil might be most appropriate for drawing an iguana, which presents a great deal of detail but is fairly uniform in color. Colored pencils might be better suited to a pheasant, where color and detail are strongly linked. Collage can be useful for representing the edge shape, overlapping, and parts-to-whole relationships of plants.

Children approach observation drawing with unique experiences and abilities, and they therefore respond to each object in highly individual ways. Once children begin drawing from observation regularly, they often select or suggest drawing objects themselves, by either bringing in items from home or choosing them from a classroom collection. As teachers assess the children's abilities and areas of difficulty, they find that further drawing objects and topics suggest themselves.

Problems and Responses

Eight- and 9-year-olds typically pass through three stages of drawing development. Problems they experience are characteristic of these stages. Children initially struggle to render individual shapes and to assemble them into a whole. Drawings at this stage appear "stuck together" from a collection of parts. Although this is seen more often with 6- and 7-year-olds, it is quite common with older children, particularly if they lack experience. If the child expresses frustration, try breaking down the task into manageable parts and focus on the parts one at a time: "What kind of shape(s) do you see? Are they the same or different? Does the (round/skinny/bumpy) shape touch another shape? Where does it touch?"

Next, children begin to focus on the object as a whole, subsuming individual shapes with an enclosing contour line. To do so, they must create a believable relationship between parts and whole. Eight-year-olds typically experience difficulty during this developmental shift. You can ease the transition by asking: "What is the line that goes around the edge like? Where does it change? How does it change?" Once this challenge has been met, children often become intrigued with indicating details, surface characteristics, and tonal variations. They may be uncertain about how to begin, especially with visually complex objects. Again, questions that break down the task can be helpful: "Do you see a pattern or design on any of the parts? How would you move your pencil to show it? Where do you see darker places? lighter ones? Where would you lean hard on your pencil? Where would you hold your pencil very lightly?"

An understanding of the child's developmental concerns provides an essential piece of a framework that allows inquiry to take place. Equally important is open communication between teacher and student, and from student to student. The teacher might ask directing or thought-provoking questions: "How will you curve the line to show that it wraps around the shell?" "When you're scared, are your eyes always big and wide?" The teacher might act as a facilitator for group investigation: "What are some ways you could move your pencil to show a stiff/furry/floppy part on your shoe?" Since 8- and 9-year-olds are increasingly social, the teacher can encourage them to rely on one another for helpful information: "Wendy also has been trying to figure out how to make her pheasant look like it's turning away—have you talked with her about how she did it?" A classroom atmosphere that encourages children to trust and share their perceptions, and to speculate freely on possible solutions to a problem, creates a setting where stimulating and instructive risks can be taken, and thoughtful, lively drawings created.

LESSON PLANS

FACES AND FEELINGS: THIRD GRADE

Objective: Expression: To learn that changes are brought about in facial features by different emotions, and to select and organize a range of lines, shapes, and marks that can be used to depict those changes.

Materials: A variety of sizes of white drawing paper, from 9" x 12" to 12" x 18", pencils, erasers, and a mirror on a stand for each child.

Room Arrangement: Children are seated at their desks, facing the mirror. This enables them to try out a range of different facial expressions before drawing, and to examine specific features while drawing.

Motivational Dialogue

TOPIC QUESTION:

> T: Have you ever noticed that people's faces change depending on how they are feeling?
>
> C: When my mom is mad, her eyes get real skinny and her mouth closes up tight.
>
> C: I can tell when my grandmother is really happy, because her face goes all soft looking.

ASSOCIATION:

> T: What parts of our faces are important for showing how we feel? Which parts change? How do those parts change?
>
> C: When my little brother gets surprised, his mouth just drops wide open.
>
> C: When I'm scared, my eyes get much rounder and look as if they are going to drop right out.
>
> T: You've been describing some very strong feelings in which your face changes a lot. What are some other feelings that can make your face change? How can it change?
>
> C: When my best friend gets mad at me, he yells so hard I can see the teeth in the back of his mouth.
>
> C: If I'm confused, my eyes squint, and my mouth feels all wrinkly.
>
> T: So what parts of your face are most important for showing how you are feeling?
>
> C: Eyes. Mouth.
>
> C: But sometimes if I'm puzzled, my eyebrows go crooked instead of straight.
>
> C: And when my sister smells something bad, her nose twitches.
>
> T: So eyes and mouth are very important for showing how we feel, but other parts of the face can change too to give us clues. What are some other feelings you can think of?
>
> C: Curious.
>
> C: Annoyed.
>
> C: Peaceful.
>
> C: Sleepy.

VISUALIZATION:

> T: Here are some mirrors. Let's try to imagine some of the feelings
> we talked about and see how our faces change. Try out two or
> three very different feelings. How do your eyes change? What
> happens to your mouth? Do other parts of your face change too?
> Do you think the whole shape of your face changes?
>
> C: If I'm pretending to be sad, the middle of my mouth goes up,
> and my eyes go down at the edges.
>
> C: When I'm looking sad, my whole face looks longer.
>
> C: If I'm peaceful, I can only see a bit of my front teeth, but if I'm
> really excited, I can see lots of teeth, even the pointy ones at the
> sides, and my cheeks look bumpy instead of smooth.
>
> T: What kinds of lines can you use to show what happens to your
> eyes when you are sad?
>
> C: Lines slanting down at the outside.
>
> C: Lots of short lines all bunched together, at the squinchy corner
> near the nose.
>
> T: How about your mouth when you are annoyed?
>
> C: A straight short line.
>
> C: A tight-looking wrinkly one.
>
> T: How do the shapes change?
>
> C: My mouth looks like a letter O when I'm surprised. When I'm
> embarrassed, it closes up and turns down at the corners.
>
> C: My eyelids go halfway down when I'm feeling suspicious.
>
> C: When I'm happy, I can't see them at all—only the eyelashes
> sticking up.

TRANSITION:

> T:: We're going to look very carefully at our own faces today and try
> to show how they change with different feelings by using differ-
> ent kinds of lines and shapes. Some of you will want to work for
> the whole class on one drawing, while others may have time to
> show several different kinds of feelings. What is the first feeling
> you would like to try to show? What parts of your face will be
> most important for showing that feeling? What part will you
> begin with? What kinds of lines or shapes will you need to use?
> Where will you begin on the paper?

SHARING AND REFLECTING:

> T: What are some of the different feelings you see in the drawings?
> How did you guess the feeling? What happens to the parts of the
> face to give you clues? What are some interesting ways people
> used the pencil to help make the feeling stronger?

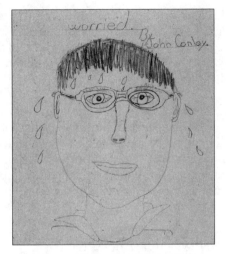

FIG. 5.1A: Worried Face,
John, Grade Three.

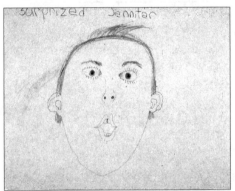

FIG. 5.1B: Surprised Face,
Jennifer, Grade Three.

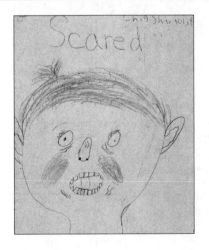

FIG. 5.1C: Scared Face,
Chris, Grade Three.

Evaluation: Did the children discover a range of interesting facial expressions to show emotions? Did they notice changes in size, shape, and location of facial features that helped to convey an emotion clearly? Did they try a range of pencil marks: dark/light, solid/broken, smooth/modulated to convey the feeling they wanted to represent?

Extensions: After children have spent some time making faces that express specific feelings and have a good sense of the changes that occur with different emotions, this lesson might be repeated as a low relief using clay. It also provides an excellent basis of information for a lesson on fantasy faces, which can be carried out using cut-paper collage to emphasize changes in shape and size, or paint to get a feel for the effects of color.

OBJECT/CONTEXT: THIRD OR FOURTH GRADE

Objective: Composition: To learn that the context of an object in a drawing has a powerful effect on the way the object is perceived, and to explore the concept of object/context relationship by selecting a real or imaginary environment from a previous drawing.

Materials: Drawings of objects from a previous lesson, pencils (colored pencils, if desired), and erasers.

Room Arrangement: No special arrangement will be necessary for this lesson, although children may enjoy sitting close together to share ideas about the drawings as they develop.

Motivational Dialogue

TOPIC QUESTION:
>   *T:*   What is an environment?

ASSOCIATION:
>   *T:*   What sort of an environment would you expect to see around the tube of toothpaste that Elizabeth drew last week?
>   *C:*   A sink, a toothbrush holder, maybe the bathtub or shower.
>   *T:*   And other very ordinary environments where you might see the tube of toothpaste?

C: In the supermarket.

C: In my suitcase, when I went to stay with my cousins.

T: If you could think of a very unusual environment for that tube of toothpaste, what would it be?

C: Being used as a baseball bat.

C: Standing in New York Harbor instead of the Statue of Liberty.

T: Which place do you notice it more?

C: In the unusual place, because you don't expect to see it there.

VISUALIZATION:

T: Today we're going to begin with the drawing you made last week of an object, and think of an environment you'd like to put that object in. What did you draw last week? What sort of environment do you think you'd like to put it in? Will it be an ordinary environment, or will it be strange or unusual? What will you see around your object? How big will the object be, compared to the rest of the drawing?

TRANSITION:

T: What will you draw first? Will it be near your object, or far away?

SHARING AND REFLECTING:

T: What story do you think Elaine's drawing tells (Figure 5.2a)? Which parts help you know? What are some of the environments that people chose for their object? Which ones seem very ordinary? Does the entire picture seem ordinary, or is there something strange about it? What has the artist done to make the environment seem unusual or strange (Figure 5.2b and c)?

Evaluation: Although many third and fourth graders will choose humorous or unsettling juxtapositions in this lesson, it is important to acknowledge the more everyday contexts that will be chosen as well. In both cases, why did the child pick that particular environment? What sort of story did they want to create about their object? How did they select and arrange the objects in the context to make that story clear to the viewer?

Extensions: This lesson is in itself an extension of a previous lesson.

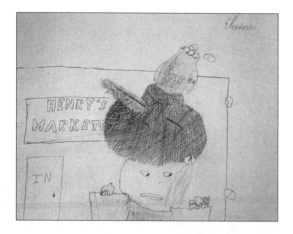

FIG. 5.2A: Shopping Accident, Elaine, Grade Four.

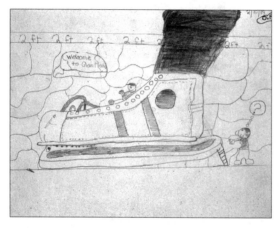

FIG. 5.2B: Skate in Giant Land, Danny, Grade Four.

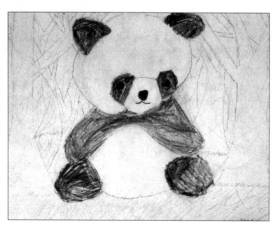

FIG. 5.2C: Panda, Meghan, Grade Four.

PHEASANT: FOURTH GRADE

Objective: Learning to Look: To learn to translate textures and patterns on a stuffed pheasant into pencil marks on paper.

Materials: 12" x 18" white drawing paper, pencils, and erasers.

Room Arrangement: A stuffed pheasant is placed on a table in the middle of the room with children sitting at tables arranged in a circle around it.

Motivational Dialogue

Topic Question:
    T: Who knows what kind of bird this is?

Association Question 1:
    T: How many different kinds of patterns do you see on the pheasant?
    C: I see stripes on the tail.
    C: The neck and wing are striped too!
    C: Some of the stripes are short, like dots.
    C: Some are thick and some are thin.

Association Question 2:
    T: Where do you see a texture?
    C: On top of the head.
    C: On the body.
    C: Under the tail
    T: What different kinds of patterns do you see?
    C: Stripes.
    C: Wiggly lines.
    C: Spots.
    T: Where do you see feathers that look soft?
    C: There are soft feathers on the back of the neck and at the top of the legs.
    T: Feathers that look rough?
    C: The feathers around the neck look rough, like scales.

Visualization:
    T: What kinds of marks will you make with your pencil to show the pattern on his neck?
    C: Short dark marks.
    T: What kind of marks will you make to show the design on his tail?

C: Wiggly marks, to show that the stripes are uneven.

C: Wide, even, dark marks.

T: Is there any place where you will use the side of your pencil?

C: I would use the side of my pencil to show the darker feathers on the chest and back.

T: Where will you make light marks?

C: I would use very light marks to show the soft feathers on the head.

TRANSITION:

T: Which way will you hold your paper, horizontally or vertically? Which texture or pattern will you draw first? Where will you put it on your paper?

SHARING AND REFLECTING:

T: How did Erin show that the feathers on top of the pheasant's head are soft (Figure 5.3b)?

C: She used her pencil very lightly.

T: Where did Wendy use the side of her pencil (Figure 5.3c)?

C: To make the very dark ring around the pheasant's neck.

T: How did Barry move his pencil to show the direction of the feathers (Figure 5.3a)?

C: The pencil marks go around the neck. On the body they go from front to back to show how the feathers grow.

Evaluation: Did students focus on the variety of textures and patterns on the pheasant? What kinds of marks did they use to depict different textures?

Extensions: Consecutive lessons could use a variety of papers to explore texture in cut- and torn-paper collage or paint to explore color and pattern.

SHELLS: FOURTH GRADE

Objective: Learning to Look: To learn that a shell can be seen as a series of edges, and as surfaces within those edges, that can be translated into lines on paper.

Materials: 12" x 18" white drawing paper, charcoal pencils, and erasers. (Option: black construction paper and white chalk may also be used for this lesson.)

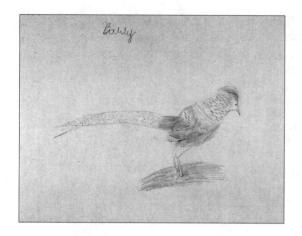

FIG. 5.3A: Pheasant,
Barry, Grade Four.

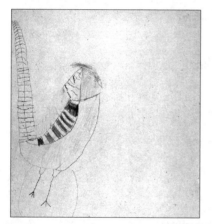

FIG. 5.3B: Pheasant,
Erin, Grade Four.

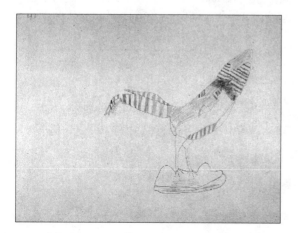

FIG. 5.3C: Pheasant,
Wendy, Grade Four.

Room Arrangement: Children are seated in groups of two with their drawing materials. A variety of shells with clear line delineation, one for every two students, are set up in a central area of the room so they can be seen clearly during the motivation.

Motivational Dialogue

TOPIC QUESTION:
> T: (Holding up one shell) Does anyone know what kind of shell this is?
> C: It's a scallop shell.

ASSOCIATION:
> T: (Indicating the edge with her finger) Let's look closely at the edge of this shell.
> C: It's kind of curved and jagged.
> T: Good. How about the edge at the bottom?
> C: It's flat and straight.
> T: If we look inside of this shell, does anyone see any edges or grooves?
> C: (Pointing) Yes, they go up and down all in here.
> T: That's right. Who can see where all of the grooves start?
> C: They all start at the bottom.
> T: And where do they end?
> C: They go out to the edge.
> T: (Holding up another shell) Looking at this shell from the side, how would you describe the top edge?
> C: It's curving.
> T: Yes, and is it smooth or bumpy?
> C: It's both. The smooth part is in the front and the bumpy part is in the back.
> T: You are looking very carefully. How about the bottom?
> C: That curves the other way.
> T: What is the back end of the shell like?
> C: It's sharp and pointy.
> T: Yes, it is sharp. Do you see any ridges on the side of the shell?
> C: Yes, they go up and down. In the front they are really close together.
> T: Do you see any other ones?
> C: I see some little ones kind of in the middle.

(This kind of questioning can be repeated using other shells.)

VISUALIZATION:

T: What kind of line would you draw to show the top edge of the scallop shell?

C: I'd make it kind of curving around with wavy points on it.

T: How about the flat edge at the bottom?

C: I'd draw it straight.

T: How would you draw the grooves on the inside?

C: I'd show them with lines that curve just a little bit starting at the bottom and going out to edges.

T: That's a good idea.

T: (Holding up another shell) What kind of line would you draw to show the top edge of this shell?

C: I would draw a wide curving line. The front I would make very smooth, but the back would have little humps.

T: How could you show the point at the back?

C: I'd make kind of a triangle.

T: Who has an idea of how you might show the ridges?

C: I would draw lines from the top to the bottom. They would be a little bit curving.

TRANSITION: (Children are called up to select the shell that they want to draw.)

T: Which part of the shell do you want to draw first? What kind of line will you make on your paper to show it?

SHARING AND REFLECTING:

T: What kind of lines did Dave use to show the outside edges of the scallop shell (Figure 5.4c)? Where can we see in Emmanuel's drawing that the abalone shell has varied and repeated grooves (Figure 5.4b)? How did he draw them? How did Bonnie show that there are ridges on the shell she was drawing (Figure 5.4a)? Did she show that the back of the shell is pointed? How would you describe the line she uses to show the top edge of the shell?

Evaluation: Were the children able to understand and identify the edges and surfaces of the shell and translate them into lines? Did the lines they used correspond to the lines they were observing? Were they interested in the task?

Extensions: Now that the children have explored edges and surfaces through the use of line on paper, these concepts could be extended in a low relief clay lesson. Children could also explore differences in edge and surface in other natural objects.

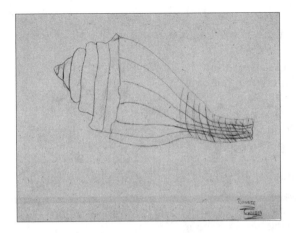

FIG. 5.4A: Shell, Bonnie, Grade Four.

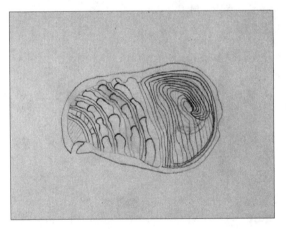

FIG. 5.4B: Shell, Emmanuel, Grade Four.

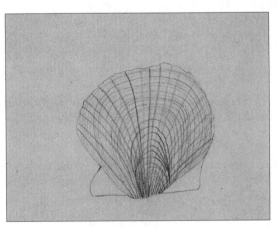

FIG. 5.4C: Shell, Dave, Grade Four.

SHOES: FOURTH GRADE

Shoes are good objects for drawing because they are familiar and important objects to children. They fit this lesson because they clearly present the problem of drawing an object that goes around in space, and they have lines and edges that are easy to follow.

Objective: Space: To begin to represent three-dimensional space by learning to translate a three-dimensional curved form into lines and curves on a flat piece of paper.

Materials: 9" x 12" white drawing paper, pencils, and erasers.

Room Arrangement: Children are seated at their desks, with their drawing materials. They are asked to remove one of their shoes, examining it visually and tactily before beginning to draw.

Motivational Dialogue

Topic Question:
>   T: What kind of shoe are you wearing today?

Association:
>   T: What kind of lines do you notice when you hold it up and look
>   at it closely?
>   T: Where do you see curvy lines? Straight lines? Looking at the side
>   of your shoe, use your finger to trace the line between the sole
>   and the upper part of the shoe. What happens when it gets to
>   the heel or the toe?
>   C: It goes around to the other side.
>   T: Can you see it go around?
>   C: No.
>   T: What does it appear to do?
>   C: Stop.
>   C: Disappear.
>   C: I don't know.

Visualization:
>   T: How will you draw the lines that go around? Will you make any
>   lines that intersect other lines? Will you draw the space where
>   your foot goes in? How will you show that it has inside and out-
>   side parts? Where will you make overlapping shapes?

TRANSITION:

    T: Which angle of your shoe will you draw? Which way will you hold your paper? What kind of a line will you draw first, a curvy one or a straight one?

SHARING AND REFLECTING:

    T: How did Jaclyn show the inside and outside of her shoe (sandal) (Figure 5.5a)?

    C: She drew edges that curve and overlap to show the way the straps go over the sole of the shoe.

    T: How did Todd show that the shoe (sneaker) curves around (Figure 5.5b)?

    C: The line that shows the toe curves around from the front edge up and back until it meets the far side.

Evaluation: What strategies did children use to show the curves, contours, and volume of the shoes?

Extensions: Consecutive lessons could continue the emphasis on three-dimensional representation with objects such as hats, backpacks, or stuffed animals. They also could spin off into the use of the expressive qualities of line, or other materials such as paint, collage, or clay.

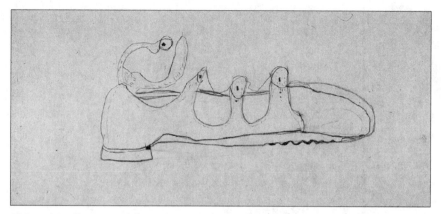

FIG. 5.5A: Shoe (Sandal), Jaclyn, Grade Four.

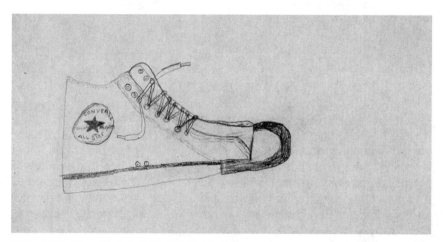

FIG. 5.5B: Shoe (Sneaker), Todd, Grade Four.

six

Fifth and Sixth Grades

DEVELOPMENTAL FRAMEWORK

Fifth and sixth graders are on the verge of adolescence. They are beginning to struggle with the inner conflict of establishing their own identities and becoming individuals separate from their families. As they begin to think about their autonomy, friends become even more significant to them and they devote much time and energy to scrambling for acceptance within one group or another. Although it is assumed most fifth and sixth graders will function at a particular developmental level, there is, as at other levels, a wide range of development in any given group. At this age, these variations can be extreme. Cognitively, some children are already thinking quite abstractly, while others are still entrenched in the concrete world. One child may be able to consider the concepts of good and evil, while another may still divide the world into good guys and bad guys. There can be extreme differences in social development as well. Some children might still be playing with action figures, while others are busy planning co-ed parties; some children already are beginning to experiment with alcohol, drugs, or sex. The teacher must teach to the level of her specific class and modify lessons for individual students when necessary.

Representation

Ten-, 11-, and 12-year-olds are comfortable using contour lines to represent edges in their drawings. Caroline is able to capture subtle variations from leaf to leaf in her drawing of a spider plant (Figure 6.2a). She makes her pencil ride along the edges of one long, curving shape and bump in and out along another. Surface texture continues to be of interest, as children are able to focus on both edge and surface in one drawing. Paul and Michael have found easy ways to make criss-cross lines to show the woven textures of the straw hats in their still-life drawings (Figure 6.1a and b). Paul's uneven pattern makes his hat appear thin and lumpy, while Michael's confident marks make his hat seem sturdier. Although Paul is still using the baseline of the paper to represent the ground, both he and Michael have assimilated the strategy of drawing overlapping shapes to show depth.

Drawings continue to become more specific and detailed. Ricky's drawing of a figure (Figure 6.8) depicts such details as wrinkles on the edge of a sleeve, shifting directions of the model's hair as part of it goes back over the head into a small elastic, a bit of a dark eyebrow, and the bolt that holds the stool together. As children mature cognitively, they begin to address how one's point of view changes the appearance of objects and places. Some 10-year-olds and most 11- and 12-year-olds are ready to tackle complicated and sophisticated issues in observation drawing.

The major shift occurring now is that children want to grapple with the problem of representing depth in a landscape, interior, or still life and volume in an object. Third and fourth graders had to move from piece-by-piece assemblage of shapes to a defining contour that enclosed a whole object. Now older and more experienced, fifth and sixth graders find that they have to consider the top, side, and bottom of an object in order to show volume. They struggle with the relationship of table to floor, floor to walls, and walls to ceiling when drawing a room, or the spatial relationships between figures when trying to show depth. Their old strategies of following a single edge as it curves around and in and out, or by overlapping to locate something in front or behind, no longer work in more complex drawings. The task now is to combine strategies or to invent new ones. Michael, a fifth grader, already is able to draw a pile of objects that are in front of and behind one another (Figure 6.1a) and to show by combining overlapping and contour that these objects are on a table surface that goes back in space. Paul deals with the problem of the table by leaving it out altogether (Figure 6.1b). Caroline makes the table go all the way around the objects, using the front edge as a baseline (Figure 6.1c). The fact that children are intrigued with this issue becomes even more obvious in a lesson focusing on composition. Tina carefully considers the way her shapes fit within the edges of her drawing paper (Figure 6.4a). At the same time, she uses diagonal lines combined with overlapping to define places going back in space. Brian is so intent on representing the long hallway receding toward the doors that it becomes the sole focus of his drawing (Figure 6.4b).

At this age, children often are fascinated with creating the illusion of three-dimensional space by using "tricks" such as one-point perspective and "shading" or modeling the form. They often ask, "How do I make it look real?" when what they generally mean is, "How do I make it look three-dimensional?" Some children may try to imitate artists' strategies, such as cross-hatching or using a "sketchy" or broken line, without really understanding them. Other children sometimes try to imitate these imitations.

It is possible to address the concerns of children at this age without teaching them specific drawing techniques. For example, the issue of perspective can be addressed by setting up a pile of boxes to draw, then asking students to look for vertical, horizontal, and angled edges. This approach helps them to discover and understand their own ways to make straight-edged objects look three-dimensional on a flat piece of paper (Figure 6.3a, b, c). This method is very different from the traditional method of teaching a one-point perspective. Children can apply that traditional formula only if they are doing certain kinds of imaginary drawings, such as railroad tracks disappearing into the distance. Asking them to draw an interior from an unusual vantage point more effectively addresses the issue of how one's point of view affects the appearance of an object or place.

Aesthetics

With consistent aesthetic education and practice, most sixth graders and many fifth graders are finally able to separate aesthetic issues from representational ones in their drawings. Rachel, a sixth grader, can represent the model's pose (Figure 6.7b), but she also is interested in conveying some aesthetic qualities in her drawing. She uses her compressed charcoal to make strong, heavy marks and big shapes that convey a sense of solidity. She confidently records contrasting surface textures, stroking with the side of her charcoal to depict the model's soft, thick hair, and making thin lines to describe stripes on her tee-shirt. In his drawing of a figure (Figure 6.6), John is beginning to explore the idea of visual tension by connecting curved and angled lines and shapes and making them press against the edges of the paper.

Children can also separate aesthetic and representational issues in their responses to each other's work. In a sharing and reflecting session, fifth graders are able to compare Caroline and Gary's drawings (Figure 6.2a and b). They can appreciate the way Gary's dark, spiky, crowded shapes create a sense of agitation, while Caroline's light, curving shapes separated by spaces suggest quietness. Children now can consciously consider the aesthetic qualities of line, shape, and texture in their drawings.

Concepts of the Material

Children at this age are able to make choices about using various materials to create line qualities and surface textures. Fifth and sixth graders can understand that a pencil is an appropriate tool for depicting contrasting shapes and edges on a plant, whereas compressed charcoal is better for showing the big, heavy parts of a figure. Michael decides to use his pencil to show various textures on the surfaces of objects in a still life (Figure 6.1a). Using light pencil pressure, he makes a soft, thin line for the feather on the felt hat. With heavier pressure, he draws thick, dark, criss-cross lines for the woven surface of a straw hat. Caroline chooses where to make light or dark, smooth or wiggly lines (Figure 6.2a). A sixth grader drawing with soft-vine charcoal can decide which parts will be smudgy and soft and which parts strong and dark. Experienced students know that collage works well for investigating overlapping and that paint is the best way to explore color. With practice and maturation, the students' use of all materials becomes both more controlled and varied. As they begin to understand the range and limits of each material, they become more fluent in expressing visual ideas.

Objects to Draw

It continues to be important to match objects with children's interests, drawing abilities, lesson objectives, and materials. Organic forms lend themselves to looser, more expressive interpretations, allowing children to practice using their new-found control over aesthetic aspects of their drawings. Plants, in particular, contain repeated but slightly varied shapes. They suggest certain rhythms that each child responds to in a different way. In a lesson emphasizing aesthetic expression, the variety of shape and texture in the leaves of several kinds of plants invites the students to make conscious choices about line and shape quality. Using pencil helps children focus on line quality; using soft-vine charcoal helps them focus on texture and tone. The figure is a complex and compelling object to use for observation drawing. It is interesting to children of all ages, but particularly to adolescents absorbed in the physical and psychological issues of self-identity.

Objects that help children explore the representation of three-dimensional space are also appropriate. Setting up a still life with a pile of hats, gloves, and tools is a way to make overlapping obvious; doing that still life with overlapping collage shapes makes the concept concrete and clear. Drawing a pile of boxes is a simple way for children to begin to grapple with the issue of representing depth and volume. Sixth graders, and some fifth graders, will be ready to tackle more complex images of interiors, landscapes, and cityscapes, using these as ways to discover new strategies for drawing.

Problems and Responses

Problems that fifth and sixth graders have in doing observation drawings are linked inextricably with their general social and cognitive developmental paths. They are very socially conscious and are likely to compare their drawings unfavorably with those of their peers. They want their drawings to "look real," and they feel embarrassed or inadequate when they do not meet their own expectations.

Responding to students' work in a way that validates their efforts is crucial. The teacher must create and support a classroom culture where a wide variety of developmental levels of work is accepted. Watching students work and listening to what they say about their work helps the teacher understand the thinking processes and intentions in each drawing. Descriptive responses help students identify successful strategies and enable them to choose those strategies in future drawings. For example

> "The way that you've used dark lines on the straw hat and lighter lines on the felt hat makes the straw hat look stiff and the felt one look soft" (Figure 6.1a).

> "The black shape inside that box makes the hole look deep" (Figure 6.3c).

> "The curving shapes of the model's arms going around the bent shape of her leg show how she was sitting, holding her knees" (Figure 6.5a).

A comment such as, "I like the way you showed that the model is sitting," is a value judgment and communicates that the student should try to please the teacher. Instead, the goal is for students to try to figure out their own useful strategies and thus increase their own sense of confidence and competence.

Four of the six illustrations of the figure drawing lessons in this chapter were made by a boy with identified learning disabilities. Ricky began this sequence of lessons by drawing generalized shapes such as those a 5- or 6-year-old might use to draw something very complicated (Figure 6.5a). The teacher was careful to validate his every effort, describing what he had done in each drawing. This helped him to become aware of the drawing strategies he possessed already and gave him the confidence he needed to work on each subsequent drawing (Figures 6.5b and 6.7a). During each figure-drawing lesson, students drew from four or five different models, allowing them plenty of time to practice focusing on each consecutive lesson objective. The entire sequence described here consisted of four lessons. By the end of the lesson sequence, Ricky was able to use contour lines and conscious variation in line weight, strategies typical of children his own age (Figure 6.8). These dramatic changes illustrate the profound effect that appropriate, nonjudgmental teacher response can have on any child's work and confidence.

LESSON PLANS

The following lesson plans do not include extensive questions and responses because they are intended for children who are experienced in observation drawing. Such children may not need to answer questions out loud. The questions posed are meant to help them focus on each lesson objective.

STILL LIFE: FIFTH GRADE

Objective: Space: To learn to translate overlapping objects in a still-life arrangement into overlapping shapes on a flat piece of paper.

Materials: 12" x 18" white drawing paper, pencils, and erasers.

Room Arrangement: Students are seated at tables arranged in a large circle. On a table in the center, there is a still-life arrangement of old hats and various containers.

Motivational Dialogue

TOPIC QUESTION:
    T: What is going to be hard about drawing this still life?
    C: So many objects, so many overlapping objects.

ASSOCIATION:
    T: From where you are sitting, which objects are overlapping? (Teacher walks around the room asking three or four children in different places.)

VISUALIZATION:
    T: How will you show overlapping shapes on your paper?
    C: Draw one in front and one behind.
    T: How do you draw "in front" and "behind" on a flat piece of paper?

C: Only draw the parts you can see.

C: Make lines stop when they hit the edge of another object.

T: Which way will you hold your paper, horizontally or vertically? Which object will be closest to the top edge of your paper? closest to the bottom edge? the sides? Will you draw the table? If so, how will you show that the objects are on the table? What will you do about the fact that there are so many objects?

C: Draw one at a time.

C: Only draw the ones I can see.

C: Draw only the ones that will fit on my piece of paper.

TRANSITION:

T: Which object will you draw first? Where will you put it on your paper?

SHARING AND REFLECTING:

T: How did Michael show that the objects were on the table (Figure 6.1a)? How did Paul show that the objects were overlapping (Figure 6.1b)? How did Michael and Caroline try to represent the table (Figures 6.1a and c)? What are some different kinds of marks people made to show soft feathers, scratchy straw, and hard metal?

Evaluation: What strategies did students use to represent overlapping objects in their drawings?

Extensions: Consecutive lessons could continue with three-dimensional space, introducing interiors, cityscapes, or landscapes, or move on to line qualities and textures using other materials to make a still life. A lesson immediately preceding this one was a collage of a simple still life; it was a way of making the overlapping issue very concrete, because cut-paper shapes can actually overlap, unlike drawn shapes, which only appear to overlap.

PLANTS: FIFTH GRADE

Objective: Expression: To learn to translate expressive qualities of plants into lines and shapes in a drawing.

Materials: 9" x 12" white drawing paper, pencils, and erasers.

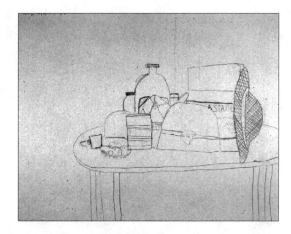

FIG. 6.1A: Still Life,
Michael, Grade Five.

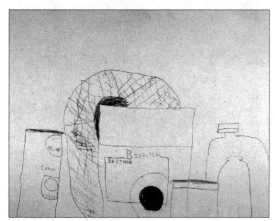

FIG. 6.1B: Still Life, Paul,
Grade Five.

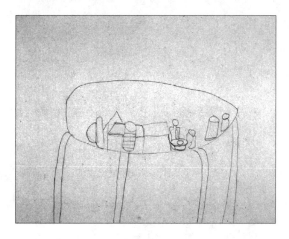

FIG. 6.1C: Still Life,
Caroline, Grade Five.

Room Arrangement: Students are seated at tables arranged in a large circle. On a table in the center are several kinds of plants.

Motivational Dialogue

TOPIC QUESTION:
  T: Who knows what kinds of plants are on the table?

ASSOCIATION:
  T: Which plants look like they have drooping, soft leaves?
  C: Some of the spider plants, the dracaena.
  T: Which ones look stiff and sharp?
  C: Some spiders, the Christmas cactus.
  T: Which ones look jagged and jumbled?
  C: The cactus.
  T: Is there a plant that looks crowded and noisy?
  C: Cactus, spider.
  T: Quiet and smooth?
  C: The dracaena.

VISUALIZATION:
  T: What kind of lines will you use to draw the spider-plant leaves?
  C: Curving.
  C: Long and short.
  C: Dark or light.
  T: Where will you use jagged, sharp lines?
  C: The cactus.
  T: Where will you use curving, flowing lines?
  C: The dracaena.

TRANSITION:
  T: Which plant will you draw first?

SHARING AND REFLECTING:
  T: Which drawing looks crowded and jumbled? Compare Caroline
      and Gary's drawings (Figure 6.2a and b). Which spider plant
      looks agitated? Which looks quiet? Why does Gary's drawing
      look agitated and Caroline's look quiet?

Evaluation: Were students able to compare and contrast qualities of shapes and edges and to translate those qualities into varying lines, shapes, and marks in their drawings? Were they able to focus consciously on the aesthetic qualities of their drawings?

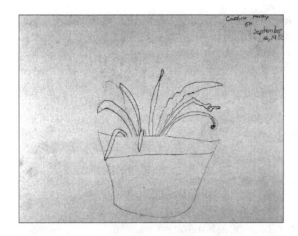

FIG. 6.2A: *Plants*,
Caroline, Grade Five.

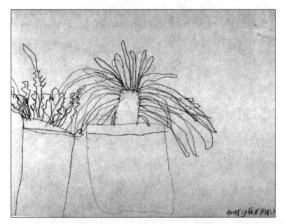

FIG. 6.2B: *Plants*, Gary,
Grade Five.

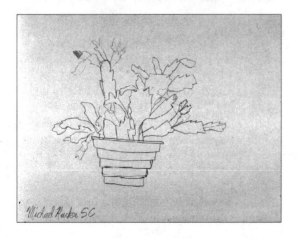

FIG. 6.2C: *Plants*,
Michael, Grade Five.

Extensions: Consecutive lessons could push expressive qualities of materials such as charcoal, paint, or collage, or they could emphasize expressive qualities of different objects, such as fruits and vegetables, musical instruments, and clothing.

BOXES: SIXTH GRADE

Objective: Space: To discover ways to use horizontal, vertical, and diagonal lines to create the illusion of three-dimensional space on a flat piece of paper.

Materials: 12" x 18" or 18" x 24" white drawing paper, pencils, and erasers.

Room Arrangement: Students are seated at tables arranged in a large circle. A pile of several cardboard boxes (6–10) of various sizes, stacked in different directions, is located in the center of the room or where everyone can easily see the pile.

Motivational Dialogue

TOPIC QUESTION:
    T: Take a look at this pile of boxes. How can we draw the whole pile?

ASSOCIATION:
    T: Where do you see straight up and down or vertical edges? Where do you see some straight horizontal edges? Where do you see some diagonal edges or edges that appear to be diagonals?

VISUALIZATION:
    T: Which way will you hold your paper, horizontal or vertical? Which edges will you show by making vertical lines? horizontal lines? diagonal lines?

TRANSITION:
    T: Which box will you draw first? Where will you put it on your paper? What kind of line will you draw first—vertical, horizontal, or diagonal? Where will you put it on your paper?

SHARING AND REFLECTING:
    T: How did Stan show that the boxes were going in different directions (Figure 6.3a)? How did Chiara show that the boxes are three-dimen-

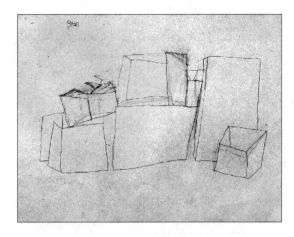

FIG. 6.3A: Boxes, Stan, Grade Six.

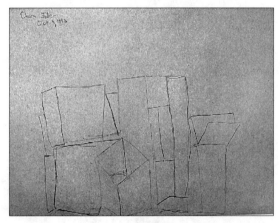

FIG. 6.3B: Boxes, Chiara, Grade Six.

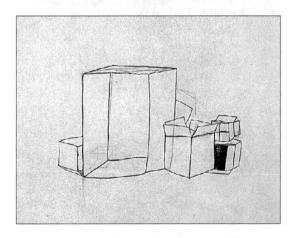

FIG. 6.3C: Boxes, Marie, Grade Six.

sional (Figure 6.3b)? Which of Marie's boxes look as if they are sticking out or have inside spaces (Figure 6.3c)? How did she make her drawing look that way? Which pile looks as if the boxes are falling and moving? Which drawing shows very still, fixed boxes?

Evaluation: Were students able to compare and contrast vertical, horizontal, and angled edges of boxes? Did they figure out how to translate those edges into lines in their drawings?

Extensions: Draw other "boxy" objects, such as telephones, televisions, or houses, or draw interior spaces, such as a corner of the classroom, a part of the hallway, or a stairway.

INTERIORS: SIXTH GRADE

Objective: Composition: To learn that the arrangement of shapes in a drawing corresponds to the pictorial space defined by the edges of the paper.

Materials: 9" x 12" white drawing paper, pencils, erasers, and drawing boards.

Room Arrangement: Children are seated in the school lobby with their drawing materials.

Motivational Dialogue

TOPIC QUESTION:
    T: Which part of the lobby do you think will be interesting to draw?

ASSOCIATION:
    T: If you are going to draw a picture of looking into the secretary's office, what will you need to include in your drawing? How can you show that you are looking into the entrance from out in the hall? What will you draw to show the hallway to the gym?

VISUALIZATION:
    T: Think about where you will draw each part on your paper. What kind of shape will you draw for the ceiling, and where will you put it on your paper? If you draw the hallway to the gym, where will you put the door shapes? What will you draw next to those? Where will you draw the wall shapes?

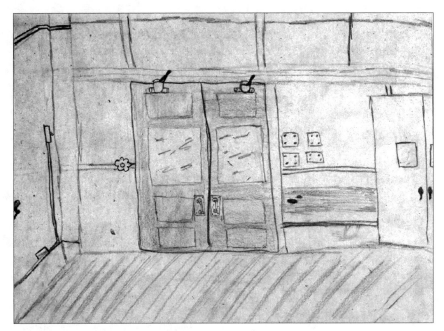

FIG. 6.4A: Interiors, Tina, Grade Six.

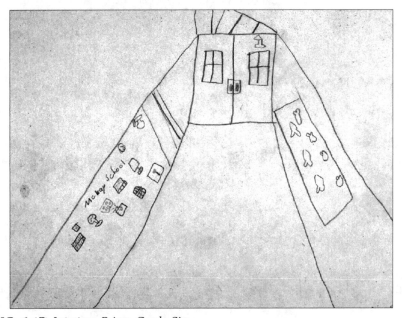

FIG. 6.4B: Interiors, Brian, Grade Six.

TRANSITION:
>   *T:*   Find the part of the lobby that you want to draw. Which part will
>   you draw first, and where will you put it on your paper?

SHARING AND REFLECTING:
>   *T:*   Which drawing has shapes that go all the way to all four edges
>   of the paper (Figure 6.4a)? Which drawing has lots of white
>   space in it? Where did Brian place the door to the gym in his
>   drawing (Figure 6.4b)?

Evaluation: Were children able to arrange the shapes in their drawing
to correspond to the parts of the space they were drawing? What kinds
of difficulties did they have with the task?

Extensions: Consecutive lessons could allow students to continue to
explore the representation of three-dimensional space in drawings, paintings, or collages of other interior and exterior spaces, cityscapes, or landscapes.

FIGURE DRAWING 1: SIXTH GRADE

Objective: Learning to Look: To look for and understand basic proportions of the human figure and to translate them into drawings, focusing on
the big shapes and how they compare in size to one another.

Materials: 18" x 24" newsprint and compressed charcoal. Compressed
charcoal is useful for the following figure-drawing lessons because it is big
and chunky, making it difficult to get involved in little details and easier,
therefore, to focus on the whole figure. The materials are the same for all
figure-drawing lessons in this sequence.

Room Arrangement: Students take turns modeling for the class, at five
to ten minutes a pose. It is important to discuss ahead of time some rules
for figure drawing—for example, the model must stay as still as he or she
can; the rest of the students must be kind to the model, not try to make
the model laugh, not deliberately make fun of the model in their drawings, and so forth. It can be embarrassing to be scrutinized in front of the
whole class.

Motivational Dialogue

TOPIC QUESTION:

    T: What are the big shapes on the model?

ASSOCIATION:

    T: Which is longer, her legs or her torso?

    C: Legs.

    T: How much longer, a lot or a little? How long are her arms compared to her torso? Where do they hit her legs? Which is wider, her head or her shoulders?

    C: Shoulders.

    T: How much wider? Which is wider, her hips or her shoulders?

VISUALIZATION:

    T: Which way will you hold your paper in order to fit on as much of the model as possible? (It's okay if the whole figure doesn't fit on the paper, as long as the parts you draw are as much in proportion to one another as you can make them.)

TRANSITION:

    T: Which part will you draw first? What size will the next part have to be?

SHARING AND REFLECTING:

    T: Everybody look at your own drawing. Did you make the legs longer than the torso (Figure 6.5a)? Does the head look like it's the right size (Figure 6.5b)?

Evaluation: Were students able to consider proportion in their drawings?

FIGURE DRAWING 2: SIXTH GRADE

Objective: Composition: To understand the figure as a series of interconnecting and interdependent angled and curved parts, translating them into contrasting, connected shapes.

Motivational Dialogue

TOPIC QUESTION:

    T: Which parts of the model are bending?

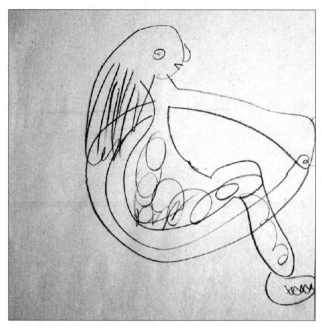

FIG. 6.5A: Figure #1, Ricky, Grade Six.

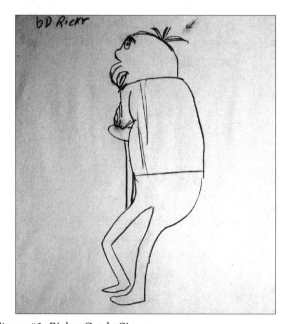

FIG. 6.5B: Figure #2, Ricky, Grade Six.

ASSOCIATION:

  T: Do you see any parts going straight up and down? straight across? Which parts are curved? Which way does the arm tilt? Is the torso straight, tilted, or curved? Which way is it leaning?

VISUALIZATION:

  T: Where will you have to draw straight shapes? Curved shapes? Tilted shapes? Where will you draw a curved shape connected to a straight shape?

TRANSITION:

  T: Which way will you hold your paper? Will you start by drawing a bent or straight part?

SHARING AND REFLECTING:

  T: Which drawing has shapes that press against the edges of the paper (Figure 6.6)? Which drawings have contrasting curved and angular shapes? Which drawings have mostly curving or mostly angular shapes?

Evaluation: Did students focus on curves and angles?

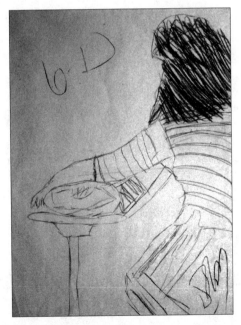

FIG. 6.6: *Figure,* John, Grade Six.

FIGURE DRAWING 3: SIXTH GRADE

Objective: Expression: To understand the figure as an object with mass and weight, and to translate that mass and weight into lines and shapes on paper.

Motivational Dialogue

TOPIC QUESTION:
>   T: Which way is the model leaning?

ASSOCIATION:
>   T: Which part(s) of the model's body is(are) supporting her weight? Which parts are touching the stool? Which parts are touching the floor?

VISUALIZATION:
>   T: How will you show which parts are heavy and which are light? Where will you make dark marks? light marks?

TRANSITION:
>   T: Which way will you hold your paper? Which part will you draw first?

SHARING AND REFLECTING:
>   T: Can you tell by looking at the drawings what was supporting the model's weight (Figure 6.7a)? What makes Rachel's figure appear to be solid and heavy (Figure 6.7b)? Which figures look light and airy? Why?

Evaluation: Were students able to respond to mass and weight? Were they able to vary their marks in response to mass and weight?

FIGURE DRAWING 4: SIXTH GRADE

Objective: Learning to Look: To look at edges and contours of the figure and translate them into lines on paper.

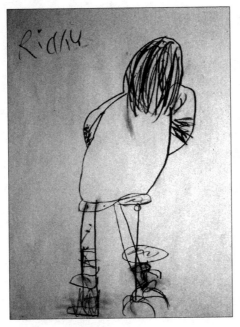

FIG. 6.7A: Figure #3, Ricky, Grade Six.

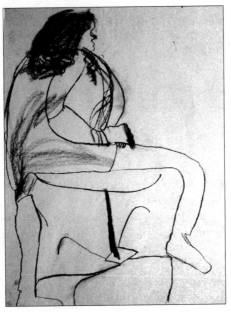

FIG. 6.7B: Figure, Rachel, Grade Six.

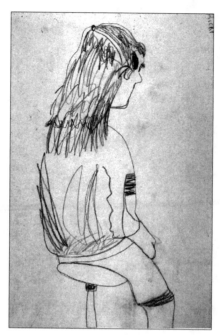

FIG. 6.8: Figure #4, Ricky, Grade Six.

Motivational Dialogue

TOPIC QUESTION:
>   *T:* Where are the smooth or bumpy parts on the model?

ASSOCIATION:
>   *T:* Look at the model's sleeve. Where is it wrinkled, and where is it smooth?
>   *C:* It is most wrinkly where the arm bends.
>   *T:* Where do you see bumpy edges? smooth edges? Where else do you see lots of wrinkles? Where is the model's body bending? Are all the wrinkles on the edges, or are some going across and around the figure?

VISUALIZATION:
>   *T:* Where will you make smooth lines? bumpy lines? Will you draw any lines going across the model's body?

TRANSITION:

    T: Where will you start your drawing, on an inside line or an out-side line?

SHARING AND REFLECTING:

    T: How did Ricky show the wrinkles on the model's shirt (Figure 6.8)? How can we tell that the shirt is softer than the pants? What kinds of lines seem to make soft edges? hard edges?

Evaluation: Were students able to focus on contour? How many were able to understand that contour can move across a form, as well as around?

Extensions: Consecutive lessons could extend exploration of the figure into other materials such as collage (mass, volume, edges, texture), paint (mass, weight, color, texture), or clay (weight, balance, gesture). Students could use drawing or other materials to explore the relationship between two or more figures, or the relationship of the figure to its environment. Another possible direction would be to explore portraits and self-portraits, using any material.

seven

Conclusion

In this book we explore the various ways teachers influence the quality of children's experiences of observation drawing. These experiences can take place within the context of a comprehensive art program or as part of regular classroom curriculum. We maintain that the following interactions are critical: encouraging development of individual drawing strategies, responding to individual thinking and problem solving, recognizing developmental issues. We maintain further that these methods are essential: making certain that materials, objects, and lesson objectives relate to one another and are suitable for a given age, creating meaningful and sequential lesson plans, and cultivating aesthetic awareness. With a teacher's attentive care throughout all these experiences, children grow confident and feel competent.

Observation drawing has widespread implications beyond the actual experiences of drawing. Teachers using the approach described in this book are helping children develop skills and attitudes relevant to other areas of study. The challenges of observation drawing engage children's thinking in concrete ways. Grappling with those challenges stimulates cognitive growth. Careful observation entails attending to detail and gathering and recording salient information. Such exercise sharpens powers of discrimination and strengthens habits necessary for rich and believable writing, and for rigorous scientific inquiry. Breaking down and reconstructing the elements of a drawing task involve problem solving, an ability essential to many other tasks. Acquiring strategies to convey meaning and the vocabulary to articulate it are fundamental to clear communication. As children become alert to aesthetic features in their own work, they can appreciate and understand those qualities in art, in nature, and in the work of others.

Drawing from observation, understood as responsive drawing, is a way of coming to know and understand the world. Children who have searched with eye and pencil for the flowing movement in the stem of the flower will not soon forget its expressive meaning, as well as its shape and structure. They will develop habits of inquiry, empathy, and analysis that go beyond the surface. They will come to believe in their power to devise an organized and expressive record of that response as well. By extension, they will learn not to take appearances simply at face value (Smith, 1990).

References

About the Authors

Index

References

Arnheim, R. (1974). *Art and visual perception: A psychology of the creative eye*. Berkeley: University of California Press.

Biber, B. (1962). *Children's drawings: From lines to pictures*. New York: Bank Street College of Education. (Original work published 1936)

Burton, J. (1980–1981). Developing minds, Parts 1–6. *School Arts Magazine:* Beginning of artistic language, *80*(1), 6–12; The first visual symbols, *80*(2), 60–65; Visual events, *80*(3), 58–64; Representing experience from imagination and observation, *80*(4), 26–30; Representing ideas in search of forms, *80*(5), 58–64; With three dimensions in view, *80*(6), 76–80.

Cicchetti, L. (1991). The child's use of materials. Unpublished manuscript.

Clark, A. B. (1897). The child's attitude toward perspective problems. In E. Barnes (Ed.), *Studies in education* (Vol. 1, pp. 283–294). Stanford, CA: Stanford University Press.

Clark, M. C. (1989). A critical examination of the literature on observational drawing in children aged five through eight. Unpublished qualifying paper, Harvard University Graduate School of Education, Cambridge, MA.

Clark, M. C. (1995). Children's understanding of genre in drawing: An examination of strategy use in observation and memory drawing by children aged five through eight. Unpublished doctoral dissertation, Harvard University Graduate School of Education, Cambridge, MA.

Colbert, C., & Taunton, M. (1985). Preschool and third grade children's development of drawing strategies to represent the perspective of a three-dimensional model. *Proceedings of the 1985 Annual Meeting of the American Educational Research Association, Arts and Learning SIG, 2* (pp. 112–117).

Dewey, J. (1958). *Art as experience.* New York: Putnam. (Original work published 1934)

Dewey, J. (1963). *Experience and education.* New York: Collier-Macmillan. (Original work published 1938)

Goldstein, N. (1977). *The art of responsive drawing* (2nd Ed.). Englewood Cliffs, NJ: Prentice-Hall.

Golomb, C. (1992). *The child's creation of a pictorial world.* Berkeley: University of California Press.

Gombrich, E. H. (1969). *Art and illusion: A study in the psychology of pictorial representation.* Princeton, NJ: Princeton University Press.

Halley, B. (1991). Responses to children's observational drawings. Unpublished manuscript.

Katz, L. (1993). What can we learn from Reggio Emilia? In Edwards, C., Gandini, L., & Forman, G. (Eds.), *The hundred languages of children: The Reggio Emilia approach to early childhood education.* Norwood, NJ: Ablex.

Kellogg, R. (1970). *Analyzing children's art.* Palo Alto, CA: Mayfield.

Lowenfeld, V., & Brittain, W. L. (1982). *Creative and mental growth* (7th Ed.). New York: Macmillan.

Luquet, G. H. (1927). *Le Dessin enfantin.* Paris: Alcan.

Piaget, J., & Inhelder, B. (1948). *The child's conception of space.* New York: Norton.

Piaget, J., & Inhelder, B. (1969). *The psychology of the child.* New York: Basic Books.

Schaefer-Simmern, H. (1961). *The unfolding of artistic activity: Its basis, processes, and implications.* Berkeley: University of California Press.

Smith, N. R. (1979). Developmental origins of structural variation in symbol form. In N. R. Smith & M. B. Franklin (Eds.), *Symbolic functioning in childhood* (pp. 11–26). Hillsdale, NJ: Lawrence Erlbaum.

Smith, N. R. (1983). Drawing conclusions: Do children draw what they see? *Art Education, 36*(5), 22–25.

Smith, N. R. (1985). Observation drawing: Changes in children's intention and translation methods grades K–6. In J. Koroscik & T. Barrett (Eds.), *Proceedings of the 1985 Annual Meeting of the American Educational Research Association, Arts and Learning SIG, 3* (pp. 47–62).

Smith, N. R. (1987). Development of the aesthetic in children's observational drawings. Paper presented at the annual meeting of the Society for Research in Child Development, Philadelphia.

Smith, N. R. (1990). Unpublished manuscript.

Smith, N. R., & Fucigna, C. (1988). Drawing systems in children's pictures: Contour and form. *Visual arts research, 14*(27), 66–76.

Smith, N. R., with Fucigna, C., Kennedy, M., & Lord, L. (1993). *Experience and art: Teaching children to paint.* New York: Teachers College Press. (Original work published 1983)

Thistlewood, D. (1992). *Observational drawing and the national curriculum.* Thistlewood, D., Paine, S., & Court, E. (Eds.). *Drawing, research and development.* Essex, England: Longman.

Werner, H. (1948). *Comparative psychology of mental development.* New York: International Universities Press.

Werner, H. (1978). The concept of development from a comparative and organismic point of view. In S. S. Barton & M. B. Franklin (Eds.), *Developmental processes: Selected writings of Heinz Werner* (Vol. 1, pp. 107–130). New York: International Universities Press. (Original work published 1957)

Werner, H., & Kaplan, B. (1963). *Symbol formation.* New York: Wiley.

Willats, J. (1977a). How children learn to draw realistic pictures. *Journal of experimental psychology, 29,* 367–382.

Willats, J. (1977b). How children learn to represent three-dimensional space in drawings. In G. E. Butterworth (Ed.), *The child's representation of the world* (pp. 189–202). New York: Plenum.

Willats, J. (1981). What do the marks in the picture stand for? The child's acquisition of systems of transformation and denotation. *Review of Research in Visual Arts Education, 13,* 18–33.

Wolf, D. & Fucigna, C. (1981). The growth of graphic representation. Unpublished manuscript. Harvard Project Zero, Cambridge, MA.

Wolf, D., & Perry, M. (1988). From endpoints to repertoires: Some new conclusions about drawing development. *Journal of aesthetic education, 22*(1), 17–35.

About the Authors

Laraine Cicchetti is a sculptor at Fort Square Studios, Gloucester, Massachusetts, and an elementary art specialist at Beverly Public Schools, Massachusetts. During the past eighteen years, she has taught preschool, elementary, and secondary school students and adults in public and private schools, museums, and art centers. She also has taught courses in art education at Wheelock and Mt. Ida Colleges.

Margaret C. Clark is a freelance illustrator and an elementary art specialist in the Melrose, Massachusetts, Public Schools. She has twenty years of experience in art education at the elementary, secondary, undergraduate, and graduate levels.

Carolee Fucigna is a teacher at the Bing Nursery School, the laboratory school at Stanford University, California. She has twenty years of experience in research and teaching in early childhood education in various preschool and college settings in Massachusetts.

Barbara Gordon-O'Connor is a painter and an adjunct faculty member in the Art Education Department, Rhode Island College. She taught art at the elementary level in Brookline, Massachusetts, for eight years, and at the secondary, undergraduate, and graduate levels in Providence, Rhode Island, for the past three years.

Barbara A. Halley is the Art Specialist and Coordinator of Visual Arts Program for grades K–12 in the Brookline, Massachusetts, Public Schools. During the past thirty-three years, she has been an art teacher in public schools for grades K–12. She has served as program administrator in Brookline, Massachusetts, and has taught in the Summer Visual Arts Institute, Boston University. In addition, she has taught undergraduate art education courses at Boston University and Louisiana State University.

Margaret Kennedy, an early childhood consultant, has spent the past thirty years teaching, directing, and supervising in a variety of preschool programs in New York, New Hampshire, and Massachusetts.

Nancy R. Smith was a painter, photographer, and the author of numerous articles and the book *Experience and Art: Teaching Children to Paint.* She co-edited the book *Symbolic Functioning in Childhood.* She served as an art educator in preschools, public schools, and university settings, including Wheelock College, Boston University, and the University of Oregon.

Index